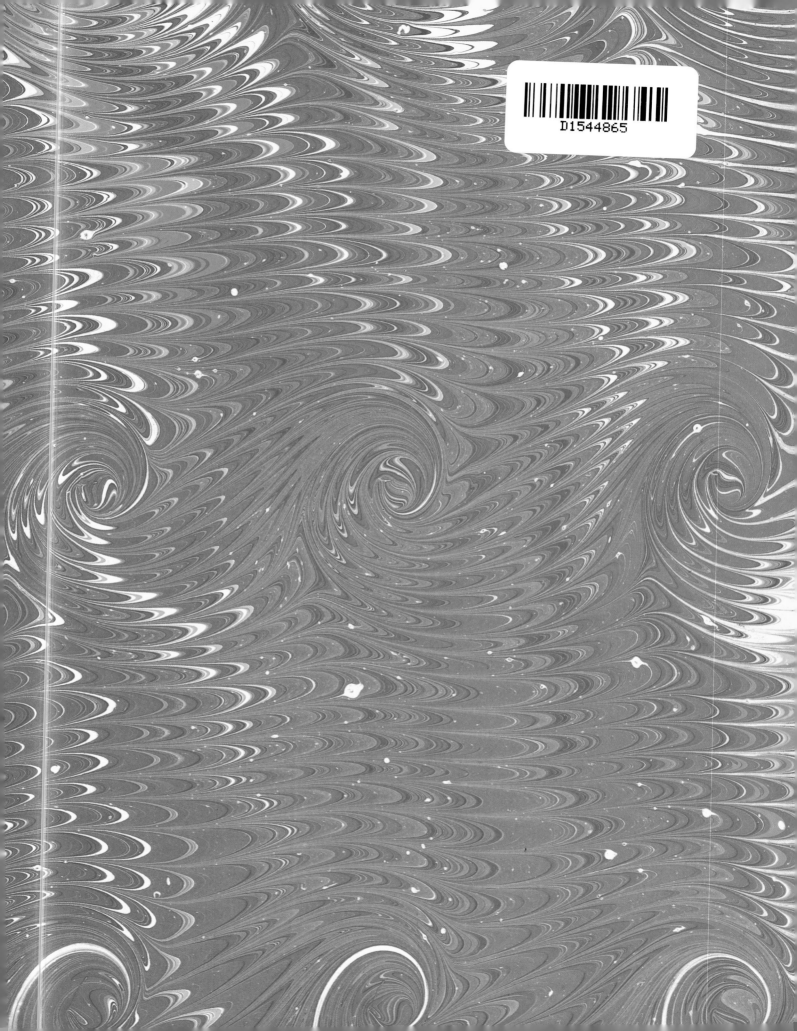

Collecting
Picture and Photo Frames

Stuart Schneider

4880 Lower Valley Rd. Atglen, PA 19310 USA

Library of Congress Cataloging-in-Publication Data

Schneider, Stuart L.
    Collecting picture and photo frames / Stuart Schneider.
        p.   cm.
    Includes bibliographical references and index.
    ISBN 0-7643-0610-3 (hardcover)
    1. Picture frames and framing--Collectors and collecting--
United States--Catalogs. I. Title.
    N8550.S38   1998
    749'.7'075--dc21

Designed by Laurie A. Smucker
Typeset in Bodini BK BT/Shelley Allegro

ISBN: 0-7643-0610-3
Printed in China
1 2 3 4

Published by Schiffer Publishing Ltd.
4880 Lower Valley Road
Atglen, PA 19310
Phone: (610) 593-1777; Fax: (610) 593-2002
e-mail: schifferbk@aol.com
Please write for a free catalog.
This book may be purchased from the publisher.
Please include $3.95 for shipping.

In Europe, Schiffer books are distributed by
Bushwood Books
6 Marksbury Avenue
Kew Gardens
Surrey TW9 4JF England
Phone: 44 (0)181 392-8585; Fax: 44 (0)181 392-9876
e-mail: bushwd@aol.com

Please try your bookstore first.

We are interested in hearing from authors
with book ideas on related subjects.

Acknowledgments

No man is an island, said John Donne. This is never more true than when you are trying to put together a book. One person's knowledge is helpful, two peoples' knowledge is wonderful, but three or more are needed to be interesting and authoritative. The author wishes to thank the following people who graciously agreed to let him photograph parts of their collections or contributed information, and without whose help this book would not have been possible.

The following people's hospitality, desire to make this a great book, and willingness to plunge into the depths of collections to find a few good pieces contributed significantly to the quality of this work:

Pam and Jack Coghlin, Joyce Frenkiel, Fran Goldstein, Georgina Hayman, John Jesse, Phyllis and Harold Perlow, Ira Pilosoff, Terry Rodgers, Susan Schwartz, Sheryl Weisbuch, The Willets Family, Zeitgeist.

Thanks also to Jeffrey B. Snyder, from Schiffer Publishing, who took some of the photographs in this collection.

Contents

Introduction

Picture frames have sometimes been called wall jewelry. They can draw the eye to and beautify a picture as they separate the picture from its surroundings. But just as with a gaudy piece of jewelry, a frame can also overwhelm the wearer and look tacky. The evolution of a frame surrounding a picture has occurred over a period of about 700 years, although common usage has only been around for about 400 years. The concept of what a frame is supposed to be also keeps expanding; it becomes more than a border surrounding a picture. The right frame pulls you into to the picture and highlights it. It accents or isolates the image. It may emphasize the importance of a picture or help connect several similar pictures. The shape and size of a frame can add to the power or message of a picture. A frame too heavy or too busy can overwhelm and distract from the picture and affects the way the picture within is perceived.

Collecting picture frames, from the 1800s and after, has only recently become popular. A few years ago, frames, with exceptions of the ornate, the early or the unusual, would be thrown in a box in an antique shop or flea market and priced at a few dollars. Those days are almost gone. More dealers are familiarizing themselves with the demand for quality picture frames and charging and getting what the market will bear.

There are now established picture frame dealers that specialize in the high end frames—those that surround paintings selling for $100,000 and up. A collector might not hesitate to spend $15,000 to $25,000 for a frame when framing a painting worth $500,000 or more. In the late 19th century, most fine painters considered one fifth to one quarter the cost of a commissioned painting as being for the frame.

Most frame collectors could be said to have come by their collection inadvertently. They did not set out to collect frames, but began exhibiting pieces from their collection in attractive frames. My interest was to exhibit my collection of 19th century photographs. I found that new frames were expensive and were somewhat distracting to the old photographs. I needed fine old frames to hold the photos and exhibit the collection. They were a challenge to locate in the right sizes, but once located, they added something to the photographs. Since that time, I have expanded to include frames that can stand on their own as art, and met others who collect the frames alone and exhibit them as their main collection.

As with any collectible, there are good frames, cheap frames, novelties, and everything in between. Through these pages you will encounter frames of many types and persuasions, although most of the emphasis is on quality frames. There are also aids for collectors of frames, such as construction, style, and materials used. There were so many frames that were not available to be included in this book, so another volume is already planned. Additionally, there were so many cheap and unattractive frames available, that they too could fill a book (I do not expect to write that book).

With the many types of frames accessible, what will you collect? Some people collect frames by period or use them as decorating accessories while others collect frames to use. There is no wrong way to collect. Most collectors start by buying frames to fit a picture and then find that they have amassed a number of frames that can stand alone as a collection. A wall of great, but empty frames, may upset some, but can be an incredible way to display a collection. Frame buyers seem to break into one of two groups: they either buy "Picture Frames," which are mounted on a wall; or "Table Top Frames," sometimes called "Photograph Frames," that stand on a table, shelf, or mantle. Let this book be your guide.

History

The idea of framing pictures may have first occurred in churches in the 1300s. Frames appeared on religious paintings and often resembled windows, arches, and architectural elements of the church. This style is often referred to as Gothic. These earliest of frames were made in Italy and Holland. They are few and far between on the antique market and are not usually available to frame collectors outside of the limited availability at some English auction houses. Most reside in museums and churches.

For the next several hundred years, frames appeared in churches and homes of the wealthy or the royalty. The average person did not have "moveable" paintings in their home. They were more likely to have a painting executed directly on a wall. Frames continued to be hand-made and too expensive for the average home.

By the 1690s, Paris was the most important frame making city. Frames were carved of wood and assembled by furniture makers. In the young American Colonies in the 18th century, frames were made from simple local woods or, for wealthy patrons, imported from England or France. These ornate frames can be seen on paintings from the late 1700s.

The most popular (and available to today's collector) types of frames were made in the 1800s and 1900s. In the early 1800s, frame makers found that the shortage of skilled carvers and the time involved in carving made ornate frames too expensive or unavailable to the average person. They began to look for ways to speed up the process.

The answer was to create wooden frames with a separately cast and applied decoration. The body of the frame was wood, but the frame's raised design was carved in a separate wooden form. This form was filled with "composition" or "compo", a putty-like material that would harden. The hardened composition was removed from the form, trimmed and then glued to the wooden frame body and decorated (usually by gilding) creating what appeared to be a hand carved gilded wooden frame. Before the industrial age of the 1860s, when water powered machines could consistently plane miles of moulding, this method saved the artist's time. It allowed the creation of more elaborate frames for less money and permitted easy duplication.

Furniture and Art Styles

Frames followed the popular furniture and artistic styles of their day. From 1800 to about 1830, an American furniture style called "Federal" was in vogue. Frames were made in the Federal style and often have columns in the inner moulding or an eagle at the top or a delicate use of applied composition decoration to the corners or edges. These are most often seen on period mirrors. Mirrors and art began to appear in middle class homes around this time. For the poorer country cousin, an American country style frame of this period may be simple planed wood with a simple gilded surface.

From 1830 to about 1850, styles became popular that were influenced by the French artists designing for Louis XV. Gold or silver leaf generally covered the entire frame. Scalloped edges with delicately applied ornamentation appeared on most expensive frames. On simpler frames, the gold or silver leaf was often only applied to the front surface and the sides were left plain. Miniature paintings were popular and frames for them were available in simple black lacquer or ornate brass embellished woods. American country style frames of this time may appear with a simple rippled or grooved wood with a painted surface or again with a painted false grain look. The painted surface was originally introduced to replicate expensive imported woods found on formal furniture.

From 1850 to the industrial age of the American Civil War, the art of the frame exhibited incredible growth. More people had paintings. Photography was becoming popular and lithographic prints were available for very little money. Inexpensive veneered wooden frames were available for the popular woodcut or lithographic prints that appeared in women's magazines. More elaborate frames exhibited natural designs in the applied ornamentation. Leaves, vines, and berries were popular. Machines, manned by moderately skilled labor, could now make what skilled artisans had formerly made by hand. Walnut was a popular wood for frame making and with the new machines, complex walnut mouldings could be easily made. A style called Gothic Revival enjoyed modest popularity. It was characterized by church architecture inspired embellishments.

During the American Civil War (1861-1865), the popularity and availability of photography, due to its low cost, appealed to every class. Frames were made by the hundreds of thousands to accommodate the outpouring of pictures. The most popular frame embellishment for the period 1860 to about 1875 was acorns and oak leaves. This acorn and oak leaf design sometimes appears into the 1880s. Walnut frames with gilded sight edges were abundant for larger photographs and prints.

Worldwide, from the 1670s to the 1870s, most expensive and high class framing required a gold leaf finish. In the 1870s, an artistic rebellion began against machine-made products. Art styles turned away from the gold look and adopted finishes that were more in harmony with the painting. This new style could be found in furniture, architecture, and art. Different "styles" emerged. Each espousing a new direction in design.

A style that lasted into the 1880s was the Eastlake style, named after Charles Locke Eastlake, an English architect who wrote a popular book entitled *Hints On Household Taste*. The book discussed Eastlake's ideas of what art, furniture, and architecture should look like. Eastlake was the inspiration, not the maker. One Eastlake principle was that wood, if painted at all, should be painted a flat color with a line introduced here and there to define the construction. Angle ornaments were acceptable at the corners. Frames in the Eastlake style can be found with delicate white incised designs on a darker background. Other embellishments might be rods, balls, spools, and spindles.

The artistically inspired works of this period are delicate and beautiful, but the production techniques were simple and easy to translate into mass manufacturing means. This went against the retreat from machine made goods. During this time, every household item was available in the "Eastlake style." Years later, after Eastlake saw the American pieces of furniture being called "Eastlake," he commented that they were a far cry from what he envisioned and he was horrified that they were being attributed to him. Eastlake styled goods were sold in Sears and other mail order catalogs and were available to every class of man or woman.

Another form—the Arts and Crafts style—used simple oak and natural finishes, usually created by hand. Metal parts were hand wrought. The Arts and Crafts movement had been building over a period of years. William Morris, an English designer, had written and spoken out in the 1870s about the industrial age furniture that was almost entirely machine made. He claimed that it was not artistic and lacked "soul." The Arts and Crafts movement was supported by the wealthy, who wanted art and could afford to commission hand-made pieces. When the wealthy became interested, manufacturers became interested. The Arts and Crafts style did not need highly skilled labor, nor time intensive manufacturing techniques. It was perfect for the masses. Again the factories began to churn out pieces made in the style and one no longer needed to be wealthy to afford artistic furnishings. Pieces in this style were made into the 1920s but the bulk of the items were made from 1900 to 1908.

The Aesthetic movement used products from nature, but added gilding or other embellishments to make them more aesthetically pleasing. Unlike the Arts and Crafts style, the designers did not believe that the only way to accomplish this was by hand. Aesthetic frames may be difficult to distinguish since they can often be classified as other styles of frames or grouped generally under the "Victorian" heading. Some Anglo-Japanese styles are called Aesthetic.

One of the strongest styles to influence art and frames was Art Nouveau. It originated in France and was exemplified in the World Exposition in Paris. It quickly spread world wide around the turn of the century. Art Nouveau stylists wanted to return to nature. The Art Nouveau style introduced flowing lines from nature such as water lilies, vines, and swirling roots and tendrils. In the straight lines of wall frames, you will not find many Art Nouveau pieces. They exist primarily in the metal table top frames, with the best being executed in bronze or copper with colored touches in enamel.

A different style, popular about the same time, was the Rustic look. In an attempt to flee from the formal, "everything must be perfect" Victorian life, a masculine response was to go to the mountains to hunt, fish, and experience nature. In the east coast of the United States, this meant the Adirondack mountains. Beginning about 1875 and continuing to about 1930, wealthy New Yorkers built splendid hunting and fishing camps in the mountains. Their craftsmen used natural wood, with the bark often in place, and pine cones and acorns, to embellish furniture and fittings for the cabin. The style soon made its way back to more formal settings in the city. Wonderful rustic frames appeared, made with pine cones and natural looking pieces of wood. Interestingly, an earlier Gothic Revival rustic style was popular in the 1840s to the 1860s when Americans were conquering wild areas of the country and making furniture out of whatever was on hand. However, it is unlikely that many picture frames were made in the Gothic Revival rustic style in the period before the Civil War.

While not actually a furniture or art style, Tramp Art frames were made from the 1870s to the 1930s. As the story goes, tramps and itinerant artists who traveled the roads and rails would gather old pieces of wood (often cigar boxes) and carve, shape, and glue the wood into useful objects such as boxes and frames. Occasionally the pieces were painted, but most were just varnished or shellacked. They sold or traded these for food and shelter. The majority are chip (also called notch) carved and made up of layers of this carved wood. Chip carving is a way to decorate wood using just a knife to cut out pieces of the wood in a repetitive pattern. It was a simple and quick method of wood carving.

During this Victorian era rebellion against machine made objects, millions of machine made frames were still being produced. As miles of moulding could be created in a day and the demand for pictures and frames was strong, manufacturers spewed out thousands of frame styles. Some are so "busy," distracting, or gaudy that it is difficult to use them today as frames for any picture. In illustrating frames in the book, it was not possible to illustrate everything. Additionally it was decided to illustrate frames that the author felt would represent the best of what is available to collectors. The number of gaudy Victorian frames has been limited. Hundreds of frames were reviewed that had gilded sight edges, velvet center bands, and busy gilded outer mouldings. Most were large and used to frame family portraits. These are readily available in almost any antique shop and usually sell for the same money as uncommon frames. As the rarer styles of frames become impossible to find, future collectors will most likely migrate to these larger Victorian pieces.

After the turn of the century, Mission style pieces, influenced by the colors and designs of the American Southwest, were popular. The American Mission style can be traced to a California church built in 1894. Gustav Stickley is the most famous Mission maker. He began showing his work in 1900. Mission pieces are usually oak and look like an extension of the Arts and Crafts movement. Mission picture frames usually have a stockier look than the earlier Arts and Craft pieces.

While most of these styles were evolving, they were being created as a "one style fits all" picture frame. If you were decorating a room in a certain artistic style, Eastlake for example, you used frames of that style to compliment your furniture. What was contained in the frame often was given little consideration or was also created to compliment the room decor. Several artists and one architect stood out as being of a different mind about what a frame should be and what it should do.

Stanford White was an architect and picture frame designer. White believed that fine paintings needed picture frames that were designed for that specific painting regardless of what kind of furniture was in the room where the painting was to be hung. He felt that the typical Victorian frame overwhelmed most paintings. White's frames contained designs that complimented the subject of the painting. His frames were to be a decorative part of the wall and each was to be different, as different as each painting for which they were designed. White revived the use of the Tabernacle frame. Tabernacle frames were the earliest of the frame styles that looked like windows and doorways. They contained architectural imagery such as sides shaped like columns with tops shaped like a mantel or a decorated shelf. White did not make the frames himself, but used New York or Boston frame makers. White designed frames can sell for many thousands of dollars.

During World War I, a "war" style appeared called Trench Art. Soldiers and itinerant craftsmen made pieces using the brass from machine gun and artillery shells. Most familiar are the hand hammered and shaped artillery shells, many which contain European battle sites and dates. Some frames of this style can be found, but they are rare. This Trench art style reappeared during the World War II. Again, shell brass was a popular medium. Occasionally, items are found made from aircraft aluminum. Again, picture frames are rarely found and actively sought by collectors.

With the end of World War I (1918), the economies of the world began to surge. People made more money and began to spend it. The economic shortages of the war were replaced by bountiful harvests and loads of consumer goods. In the 1920s, a new art form captivated the world. It was the Art Deco style and the era of the flapper. Early Art Deco designs resembled the flowing artwork of Art Nouveau pieces, but with a more formal execution or applied to more mechanical items. In the 1930s, the Deco style further embraced the machine age and streamlined everything mechanical, while keeping the formal or cubic nature of the item. Black, white, and silver were popular finishes. Bronze, rather than gold, was often used as a finish. Art Deco frames were made to compliment Deco interiors. Some of the simpler frames of this time used strips of colors, such as blues or greens, in their center bands.

From the end of the Deco era and to the beginning of World War II, frames made for home use became more utilitarian. Fancy table top frames were still being created for wedding pictures, but thousands of inexpensive stamped metal frames were available for photographs. Most exhibit very little stylistic interest. During the war years some inexpensive frames sported patriotic motifs. Many metals were destined for use by the military so frame makers had to make due with glass, plaster and other non-essential goods for their table top frames. Wooden wall frames were generally unexceptional and were soon replaced by simple metal frames. The age of the great frame was over.

The Table Top Frame

The table top frame made its appearance in the 1840s as the daguerreotype case. The daguerreotype, a photograph on a silver plated copper plate, was the successor to the miniature painting, popular in the 1810s to 1840s. Before photography, the only way to capture a person's likeness was in a silhouette or painting. The paintings were expensive and time consuming when done by a talented artist and the silhouettes did not capture what the face looked like. A photograph was much faster and substantially less expensive. Miniature paintings were hung on the wall. The daguerreotype, done on a mirror-like surface, needed to be tilted just right to view it, therefore it was difficult to get the viewing angle correct when hung on a wall. The daguerreotype was set into a case and the case was placed on the table.

In the 1850s, the Ambrotype photograph replaced the daguerreotype. About 1860, the tintype and paper photographs, mostly Cartes Di Visites (CDVs), began to replace the earlier photographic methods. CDVs were made by the millions and very reasonably priced. Special albums were made to hold them and some table top CDV frames began to appear. About 1870, larger numbers of table top frames emerged. The table top frame "craze" took off about 1880. Soon, thousands of table top frames appeared.

In Victorian society, wall and table frames were the way to exhibit photographic or small painted portraits. Heavy silver and gilded brass table frames were popular. The standard place in the house to exhibit photos was on the fireplace mantle. In time, the mantle became overcrowded and new places were sought for the photos. An overmantel was created to hold more pictures. As the overmantels became encumbered, tables, easels and shelves were used to hold the overflow. The cluttered look of Victorian rooms was probably caused by too many table top picture frames and their accompanying places of display.

At the turn of the century, some popular types of table top frames used interlinking, flattened brass rings, or hammered curved brass wire to make up the border of the frame, while others were made in highly decorated cast metal. The style is still so popular that many cast metal Art Nouveau style frames are being reproduced today.

Wooden Picture Frame Terminology

Most wall frames made after 1850 will have mitered corners. The miter joint is the simple joining of two mouldings cut at a 45° angle, then nailed and/or glued together to form a right angle. The two right angles are joined to form the picture frame.

A variation on the miter joint is the splined miter joint where a tapered groove is cut into the right angle miter joint and a third piece of wood is inserted to bind the two and give the joint strength.

Other frames are made with a lap joint, where the ends of the moulding are squared off, but the surface of one (halfway down) and the back of the other (halfway up) are cut away. The two pieces are overlapped and glued. These tend to appear more often on pre-1850 frames or large frames that need more support. Sometimes the lap jointed frame will have a mitered veneer on the surface.

A variation on the lap joint is the tongue and groove (lap) joint where a gutter (the groove) is cut into the center of one end of a piece of moulding and the front and back of the other moulding is cut away leaving a flat finger (the tongue) projecting which fits into the groove. The tongue is glued into the groove. Most oil painting canvas stretchers are made this way. The frame is very stable and the joints are not subject to distortion.

Older frames are often complex—that is, they are made up of several layers of frames, nestled one inside the other (a frame within a frame). Many have two layers, some may have up to five layers. Each separate layer is usually a complete frame in its own right, except that the inner layers do not to have their outside edges finished, since that edge is covered by the next outer layer. This can be confusing to anyone looking at pre-1850 frames as many simple frames were made with a single layer, such as the inexpensive American frames used to hold (Currier and Ives type) lithographs. Most current wooden frames are made with one layer, since several layers are more expensive to make and assemble. The modern single layer gives the impression that it is composed of several layers.

Frames have an inner moulding, called the "lip," "liner," or "sight edge," or sometimes simply "sight," which is the moulding closest to the picture. Next out, are one or more "center mouldings" also called "center bands." The outside portion of the frame is the "outer moulding" or "edge moulding."

The width of the moulding is the distance from the outside edge to the lip. For most of the frames illustrated, this number can be obtained by subtracting the overall frame dimension from the picture size and adding a quarter to a half inch to account for the ledge that holds the picture in place.

"Beading" or "Pearls" are decorative moulding trim that resembles beads or pearls. They can be found on any level of the moulding.

"Rods" are decorative pieces added to a frame, usually found in the center mouldings.

"Panels" are flat or sloping areas of the frame, usually without decoration.

A "cove" is a scooped out (as if an ice cream scoop removed that part of the wood) area between the sight edge and the edge moulding.

"Ogee" is somewhat opposite of a cove. Ogee frames have a smooth mound that leads away from the picture between the sight edge and the edge moulding that curves up, shaped like the letter "S". Ogee frames are usually veneered. The veneer can be simple mahogany or a finer grade of wood with a burley or exceptionally nice grain design such as bird's eye maple.

"Veneer" is a thin layer of well grained or expensive wood that is glued over the less expensive wood that makes up the base of the frame. Mahogany may be the most popular veneer.

Oval frames—Oval frame making is more complicated than square or rectangular frame construction. Early solid wood ovals were expensive and time consuming to make. Examine the construction and see how the wood is joined and worked and the smoothness of the finish. In the 1870s, frame makers began to look for ways to simplify oval frame making. One way was to cut a roughly finished frame, coat it with composition or gesso and then paint it. As wood working machinery became more sophisticated, ovals were standardized and made as a single layer of frame rather than the earlier multi-layered frame.

The woods used to make the surface of a frame can give an indication of the frame's age. From 1810 to 1840, cherry and maple finishes were popular. Bird's eye maple—maple with darker crescent-like shapes throughout the wood—was highly prized. These woods are usually found as veneers. The underlying wood of the veneered frame may be basswood, poplar, or pine. All three are easy to work with hand tools and cost less than most other woods. Mahogany was popular from the 1830s to the 1880s. The best early mahogany was tight grained and has a shimmering depth to it, similar to an opal or a piece of the semi-precious stone called catseye. As the old growth of mahogany disappeared and newer growth mahogany became available, the wood's grain became very open. Generally a wood filler is used with new growth mahogany to fill in the wide grain. Mahogany is usually found as a veneer. Walnut was a popular wood in the 1860s to late 1870s. Many walnut frames from this period are solid walnut. As the great stands of walnut trees became scarce, walnut became too expensive to use as anything except veneer. Oak became popular in the 1880s and its use continued until about 1920. Oak was a harder wood to work with, but was abundant and very stable.

Many wood frames have decorative features. The decoration is usually made of "Composition" or "Compo." Compo starts out as a putty-like material and then hardens. It makes up much of the raised decoration on ornate frames. To make applied compo mouldings, the frame maker would take a glob of compo, lay it into a carved wooden form, and cover it with a piece of wood. The form goes into a press and after pressing, takes the shape of the mold. It is allowed to firm up, then is removed and applied to the wooden frame, hardening like stone in a day or two. Another way to use compo was to apply a layer of compo to a strip of moulding or a completed wooden frame. The moulding was then run under an incised patterned wheel and the pattern was transferred to the compo covered moulding. A simple design could be run through quickly, while an intricate or deep design would move more slowly. Originally the wheels were wooden, but about 1920, frame makers began using a brass wheel which would last longer. Composition, due to its elastic nature when soft, could have some design under cutting similar to hand carved wood.

One recipe to make a pound of Compo is as follows: a quarter pound of flake carpenter glue is dissolved in eight oz. of boiling water and a quarter pound of yellow rosin is heated with one oz. of linseed oil. The rosin and glue mixtures are combined and a half pound of whiting is stirred into it until it is the texture of putty. Shredded cloth or paper is sometimes added as a binder. The mixture hardens in twenty-four hours.

Another frame making material is "Gesso." Gesso is a creamy glue-like material. It is made like Compo, but liquid hide glue is used rather than flake glue and the rosin is left out. Gesso is painted on the frame to give a smooth surface, hide defects or to join the decorative compo decoration to the frame. It accepts paint very well. It is also used to coat stretched artist canvas before painting.

If the frame is to be gilded, another material, called "bole," is used. Bole is a fine clay-like product that is applied beneath gold leaf to give a smooth surface with which to bond and lend color to the transparent leaf. Different colored boles will give gold leaf a warm or cold tone. Bole is usually red or blue/gray. French frames often have a pink bole beneath the gilding.

Gold leaf and bronze powder were popular finishes for the whole frame or a portion of the frame. Gold leaf is pure gold that has been hammered into extremely thin sheets, so thin that they are slightly transparent. To put the gold leaf finish on a frame, a gilder would smooth the bole surface of the frame and then paint it with a layer of sizing glue. The leaf was laid on the sizing and pushed into place with a fine brush. The application of gold leaf is called "gilding." It could be burnished (rubbed with a smooth, hard object) to give it a brilliant shine or left alone for a rich gold finish. It was usually coated with varnish to protect the delicate gold surface. Old gold leaf surfaces may have darkened over time due to the aging of the varnish.

There are two major types of gold leafing—oil gilding and water gilding. In oil gilding, the sizing "glue" that holds the leaf to the frame is an oil and the final finish is matte rather than glossy. In water gilding, the sizing "glue" that holds the leaf to the frame is water based and the final finish is shiny gold. Water gilding is the more expensive and time consuming process. In many early to mid-19th century frames, the surface was gilded and the edges were painted with bronze powder or left unfinished to cut costs.

"Gilt" is a bronze powder finish. Bronze powder was an alternate finish as it was less expensive than gold leaf and as such, was considered to be a lower quality finish. Bronze powder was mixed with sizing, applied over sizing or mixed with banana oil. The finish resembles gold leaf, but lacks the surface of real gold. At the turn of the century when electric lighting was being installed in homes, the gilt finish began to be used on higher quality frames. The gold leaf finish was often too shiny and distracted the eye from the picture within.

One can find other finishes that resemble gold such as silver leaf or aluminum leaf that has been covered with orange shellac. There is a certain look to an 1840s frame where the shellac has worn away and the silver has begun to tarnish. It is a pleasing and sought after look. Silver leaf finishes occasionally were left as a silver finish.

Popular finishes during the 1860s to 1880s were the faux bois (imitation wood), faux marble, and faux tortoise. The tools used to apply these finishes were graining brushes, feathers, sponges, bundled rags, and occasionally a paint brush. They were designed to imitate earlier and more expensive surfaces on wood. In the 1700s, actual tortoise shell was heated and glued to frames. As mentioned earlier, wood graining finishes were popular in the 1830s to 1850s as a country style finish. The wood grained effect became popular again about the turn of the century.

Table Top Terminology

"French Style" refers to a frame that has a ribbon design at the top and was probably made in France. (Note: the metal on frames made in France is often more brittle than that found on similar frames made in other parts of the world.)

"Easel back" refers to a support that is attached or swings out from the top rear of the frame.

"Pivot stand" or "swing arm" refers to an arm that is attached to the back bottom of the frame and swings out to make the frame stand upright.

Photographic Terminology

The earliest photographs are usually found as Daguerreotypes. "Dags," as they are called, were made from 1839 to about 1860. They are identified as a photo on a highly polished (mirror-like) silver plated piece of copper. They were usually cased. The surface of the Dag was delicate so it was protected by a brass mat and a cover piece of glass. Around 1850, a "preserver" was added. The preserver was a thin brass frame that held the Dag, mat, and glass in place. As fashion dictated over the years, many Dags were taken, by their owners, from their original case or mat and replaced in a new case or mat.

The next popular process was the Ambrotype. Ambrotypes were made from 1854 to about 1865. They are identified as a photo on a glass plate. The glass can be a dark ruby red in color or clear and backed in black to make the photo appear as a positive.

In photographic frames for Daguerreotypes, Ambrotypes, and Tintypes, the standard picture sizes are: Ninth plate, 1.5 x 1.75 inches; Sixth plate, 2 x 2.5 inches; Quarter plate, 2.75 x 3.25 inches; Half plate, 4.5 x 5.5 inches; and Full plate 6.5 x 8.5 inches.

The small hinged case that held the Dags or Ambrotype and its preserver was originally a leather covered pressed board case. The first cases (William Shew is believed to be the inventor) were covered with plain leather. Soon manufacturers began to decorate the case by embossing the leather. Early designs show baskets of fruit, fountains, deer in the garden, romantic scenes, and other period imagery. Some of the cases were made for specific photographers and bear their name or mark. The mark could be on the outside of the case, impressed into the velvet on the inside, or stamped on the brass mat. John Plumb, a well know photographer, had a basket of fruit and flowers on his cases. Mathew Brady had his name stamped on the outside of some cases.

Another form of case appeared about 1854. These were called "Union" cases and were made of a thermoplastic material. This hard rubber-like material is often mistakenly called Gutta Percha. The material was actually made of shellac, sawdust, and carbon black which was pressed into a mold and heated. Most of these cases were decorated with designs similar to those covering the leather cases. During the American Civil War, some cases had patriotic or military scenes on the outside.

Tintypes, sometimes called ferrotypes, were generally made from about 1860 to the 1890s with some actually being made into the 1920s. The Tintype photo is on an enameled or japanned tin plate. It can be found in Ambrotype sizes as well as CDV sizes. Tintypes were sold by the millions. Tintypes made in the early 1860s were usually sold in the same cases that held ambrotypes and daguerreotypes. From the mid-1860s they were offered in CDV size and were usually stored in an album.

Carte de Visite, or "CDV", refers to a photo 2.25 x 3.75 inches on a card—2.5 x 4 inches. Pronounced "Cart Di (as in "did") Vizeet", these were albumen photographs. The CDV was invented in France in 1854 and made its appearance in the United States around 1860. Numerous frames and albums were made to hold CDVs. It is said that over 100,000 CDVs of Abraham Lincoln were made for his 1860 presidential campaign. Millions were made of the general population. CDVs were produced from 1860 to 1885. Most were made from 1861 to 1875.

Another popular frame size was designed to hold cabinet cards. Cabinet card refers to a photo 3.75 x 5.5 inches on a card that is 4.25 x 6.5 inches. They were introduced in 1867 and made until just after the turn of the century. Most were made from 1876 to 1896 and would have appeared in albums and table top frames.

After the cabinet card, there was very little standardization of photographs, though a popular mount for the photographs was a gray card about 5 x 7 inches. The photo was usually smaller than the mount. These photos were usually exhibited in a frame rather than an album. Around 1912 photographic postcards began to appear. Special frames were created to hold one or more postcard photographs.

Dating

Collectors love specific dates, but take each frame's date with a period of leeway since most frame styles were made for a period of years.

When you first pick up a frame, look at the style. Does it look like Mission Oak, Art Deco, Art Nouveau, 1860s walnut, early veneer, or some other style? Look at the surface of the wood or other material. Some wooden frames have been refinished or re-varnished and they may not look old. Others may just look old. Within the last thirty-five years, frame manufacturers have found a market in older styled frames and have begun to make the fronts of these frames look as if they could be a hundred years old.

Don't overlook an old refinished frame. A well refinished piece may be as valuable as one with an original finish. Some incredible woods were used in frame making 150 years ago. With time, the varnish on the surface may have darkened enough to obscure the wood's character. Closely examine old dark wood frames that may actually look wonderful when the old varnish or shellac is removed.

Next, turn the frame over and look at the back. Old frames should show old construction. Is it made up of several layers? Now look at the color of the wood on the back of the frame. It should be darkened with age. Look at the edges. They may not darken as much as the face of the frame. Check to see if they are painted or finished like the face of the frame. Unfinished edges may indicate that you are looking at only a piece of a multi-layer frame. A wooden back board or old nails do not guarantee an old frame, but is an indication that the frame could be old. What is the image in the frame? It is certainly easy enough to change pictures in a frame, but the old picture may help to date the frame or the picture may contain a name and date, more indications of age.

Older table top frames may give an indication of age from the type of back and stand—easel, wire, paper or velvet covered cardboard, or swinging arm stand. Look at the fronts and backs of lots of frames, even new ones. They need not be frames that you are interested in. As you become more familiar with the materials, styles, and construction, you will be in a better position to estimate the frame's age within a range of years. After a while, you will get a "gut" feeling if the frame is not right or is an incredibly old frame at a true bargain price. Ask the person selling the frame what they know about it. They may have no idea or they may be able to tell you a great deal of information.

Silver and brass darken with age and can be shined up with polish or a buffing wheel. Where the silver or brass is on tortoise shell, leather, or wood, look closely at the areas under the silver overlay for signs of dirt, wax, or polish buildup. When the underlying area is as bright and shiny as the uncovered area, the age of the frame should be suspect. These areas should show some of the effects of nearly 100 years of tarnishing and polishing. Keep in mind that a simple period frame can be embellished by a modern craftsman with silver or brass fittings nailed into place.

Frame Care and Repair

Most frames will profit from a cleaning. Depending upon the material, you can use an ammonia and water solution to remove years of dirt and grime. Use a damp sponge and clean a small section of the frame. Once you have ascertained that the finish is not coming off, you can be a bit more aggressive in your rubbing. Dry immediately and make sure that the solution does not run into any picture that is framed within. Touch up any nicks or dings with gold paint or a brown or black magic marker. These will distract the eye from the minor damage. For more major damage, you will need additional supplies. A bit of wax or furniture polish will usually bring up the shine.

As with any repairs, start on a frame that you will not regret destroying. You will get better with practice and will learn what can and cannot be properly repaired within your skill level.

If gesso or composition pieces break off a frame, save them and re-glue them back in place with a good wood glue. You can buy a liquid rubber or molding liquid that can be used to recreate lost parts of a frame. This and other materials mentioned here should be available in hobby shops or artist supply catalogues. The remaining parts of the frame should be coated with a very light coat of vegetable oil. The liquid is painted onto the frame and allowed to dry. Continue painting on layers until the form is thick enough to hold its shape when taken off the frame. Use plaster of paris or a similar product to cast a new part. When hard, trim it with a knife and fit it into place on the frame. Once you are satisfied, glue it in place, let the glue dry, and fill in the gaps with gesso. When dry, you can gild the repair, paint it with gold paint or bronze powder. This procedure is time consuming and does not pay for an inexpensive frame.

Resizing frames is possible with a good miter saw and frame cutting jig. The saw will be dulled by the composition material after cutting through several frames, so learn how to properly resharpen the saw. Saw slowly and let the motion and weight of the saw cut the molding. Do not bear down on the saw or the cut will not be straight.

Missing glass can be obtained at most hardware or glass and paint stores. Tell them that you want glass for framing. Try to obtain the thinnest glass that will do the job. If you are bothered by reflections you can buy anti-reflective glass. Most will dull a picture. You can also buy special anti-ultraviolet glass that will protect any photographs or colored prints that are hung in a very lighted area. Clean glass with ammonia and water and wipe with a piece of newspaper. The newspaper will remove most streaks.

Loose joints in frames can be repaired by forcing glue into the joint and clamping it in a framing jig. If you want to hammer in additional nails, drill a thinner hole first or the wood may split.

Collecting Frames

For the collector, there is an imposing amount of information to digest about picture frames. A good collection reflects the tastes of the collector. Here are some general thoughts about collecting picture frames.

Condition—A composition covered or veneered piece in mint condition may be worth several times more than one in damaged condition. Damage may be a major problem. An item with a piece missing may be worth 25% of one with the piece present. Missing veneer or composition can often be replaced. The repair may be costly. The items in this book are priced in excellent condition although the actual piece shown may vary from good to perfect.

Availability or "Will I ever find another?"—Some items are always available at antique shows or specialized dealers. At this time, the collector can easily find simple walnut wall frames from the 1860s and 1870s or cast iron table top frames from the early 1900s. Ask yourself, is just a matter of dollars to acquire an example or is this a once in a lifetime chance to find that item? With a once in a lifetime item, condition should not be the major determining factor. Many items are rare. On those items, you may never get another chance to buy one and the person behind you may be waiting for you to put it down so that he or she can buy it.

Style—Will all of your frames be of a certain style or material or will you collect everything that grabs your attention? If your furniture is Mission oak or Eastlake, you may want to stay with that style of frame for your artwork. You can collect by theme. There are Victorian photo frames with hearts and cherubs often called "Wedding" frames and originally made for pictures of the bride and groom. These are a nice way to show off family pictures. There are many styles of folk art frames. Tramp art, hand decorated, rustic, and match stick are a few to look for. An entire collection can be created with tramp art frames which can be dated from shortly after the American Civil War to the 1930s.

A popular style of wood decoration was pyrography. In pyrography, the design is burned or branded into the wood of the frame with a soldering iron style tool. Much of the pyrography work is by talented home artists. The home craftsman could buy a stencil and transfer the design to the wood. He would then burn along the lines to create the design.

Reproductions and Fakes—Crocodile, alligator, and snake skin covered frames can be found in much greater abundance than were originally created in the 1920s and '30s. Apparently, some savvy English craftsman are buying up old luggage, belts, and other old reptile skin covered pieces and refitting them to rather ordinary period frames. The end result has all the appearances of age, including hefty prices, but the items are fantasy pieces. There are some exquisite "turn of the century" frames made of tortoise shell and sterling silver that are available in London antiques markets. They sell for $800 to $3,000. They look wonderful, but have a very new look to them. It is believed that they probably are period frames but from the sampling that has been seen, they show almost no signs of use or cleaning.

Demand—Table Top Frames: The most popular table top frames have space for a rectangular picture that is 4 x 6 inches. Frames for photos that are smaller than 3 x 5 inches are also in good demand. Table tops with picture space larger than 6 x 9 are not as popular but seem to be gaining in popularity. Oval picture frames are not as highly sought as rectangles. Victorian wire frames are more desirable than most Victorian cast metal frames.

Wall Frames: Many collectors currently chase high quality gilded frames from the 1800s and known frame maker's work from the first several decades of the 1900s. Well made folk art frames are grabbed up quickly when offered by dealers. Quality frames from the 1870s are gaining in popularity. Art Nouveau and Art Deco frames are popular.

Buy the Best—In comparing frames to other collecting fields, it is expected that prices will continue to rise. Higher prices may be a blessing in disguise. Some people have no incentive to sell a piece for only a few dollars, but if they can get "a lot of money" they will sell it. You will pay more but you will get a frame that you may never have another chance to own. Collections can be put together for very little money, but, as has been proven true in every field of antique collecting, the best pieces in the best condition have held or increased in value at a greater rate than the more common pieces. Buy the best that you can afford. Remember, you will rarely regret having paid too much for an item, but you will always regret the good pieces that got away.

Locating items—Frames can be found at garage sales, antique stores, antique shows, and flea markets. There are specialized frame dealers in some larger cities and frame auctions at some of the auction houses in England.

Valuing Frames

Valuing frames can be difficult. A flea market may sell a frame for $10 to $100. A specialized frame dealer who restores frames and can resize them to the customer's picture may sell a similar frame for five to twenty times that amount. These specialists are the place to shop when you need a frame in an exact size. If you can resize frames using frame making tools, you may be able to save money by finding a larger frame and adjusting it to your picture. A collector who is attempting to find a certain frame for his collection may value that item many times higher than another person who already has one. That collector might be willing to pay $500 for one piece, but would he buy a second or a third at the same price? It depends upon who is buying, the availability, and how badly he wants the item. Due to increased competition, prices are steadily moving upward.

The items in this book are valued by people who sell and collectors who buy. Values are given in ranges and I have tried to give values that dealers can sell at and collectors will buy at. The dealers have not set "top dollar" prices and the buyers are not paying "through the nose." It is believed that these are the fair ranges that the frames usually trade in. Keep in mind that the person that you deal with may not follow these "rules."

It is often said that a price guide is out of date the moment that it is published. Do not let that affect your use of a value guide. A value guide is comparative. It allows you to compare two items to determine if they are of comparable value. It is useful in buying and trading and it can help give you a feel for the rarity of a piece.

Remember, two is a coincidence, three is a collection. Happy hunting!

Wall Frames

CARVED AND PAINTED WOOD, ca. 1820. A small American frame carved of one piece of wood. The front oval is raised above the background of the face of the frame. It would have held a miniature painting. 4 x 5.25" with a picture size of 2.75 x 3.75". Value $225-$275.

MINIATURE PAINTING, ca. 1810. Lacquered wood frame with a brass lip. This wall hanging frame was probably made in England. The style was popular and was used from 1790 to about 1840. 5.25 x 5.75" with a picture size of 2.5 x 3.25". Value $125-175.

PINE, ca. 1820. An early American, mitered corner, planed pine frame with raised rib with an ogee shape. 18 x 22" with a picture size of 11.5 x 16". Value $400-$450.

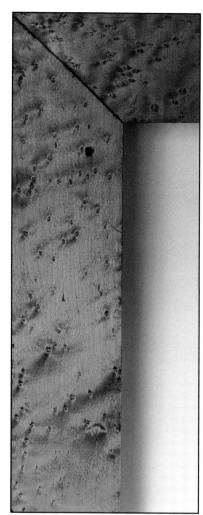

BIRD'S EYE MAPLE, ca. 1825. A strongly grained wooden frame that uses the finest wood as a veneer. The strong "eyes" give the frame a sense of depth or dimensionality. 20.25 x 22.25" with a picture size of 15 x 17". Value $350-$450.

BIRD'S EYE MAPLE, ca. 1825. A great American frame with a maple veneer. Before the frame was assembled, the four pieces of the sight moulding were set into a groove in the outer moulding. It would have held a small painting. 7 x 8.25" with a picture size of 4.75 x 3.25". Value $350-$400.

CHERRY, ca. 1830. A simple wooden frame with a gold leafed sight edge. 13 x 15" with a picture size of 10 x 12". Value $350-$400.

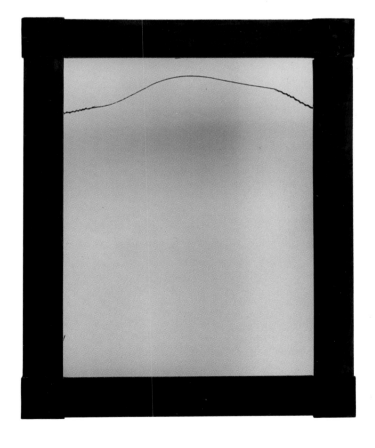

OVERLAPPING CORNER CONSTRUCTION, ca. 1830. A well made, fine grained veneered frame that is constructed with overlapping corners. The frame maker has added a darkened square block of wood to each corner to remove the distracting lines of the overlap. The wood, darkened with age, appears to be walnut or mahogany. 13.5 x 16.5" with a picture size of 10.5 x 13.5". Value $350-$400.

GILDED WOOD, ca. 1830. An American frame with a gilded finish. The outer edges are left ungilded. The framer has used a combination of water gilding to obtain a shiny gold sight edge and an oil gilding in the rest of the frame to obtain a matte gold finish. 18.75 x 21.5" with a picture size of 16.25 x 19". Value $350-$425.

PAINTED WOOD, ca. 1840. An American frame with simple mitered corners and a painted finish made to resemble tiger striped maple or mahogany. 4.5 x 5.25" with a picture size of 3.5 x 4.25". Value $100-$130.

WALNUT AND BRASS, ca. 1835. A beautiful small French walnut frame. The glass is curved. The style of brass center swirl on a painted, plain back can occasionally be seen on late eighteenth century French miniature paintings. The extra embellishment indicates that it is later than eighteenth century. 5.25 x 5.25" with a picture size of 2.5" in diameter. Value $200-$225.

PAINTED WOOD, ca. 1840. A small American frame with a painted veneer. The back shows that the frame is made of overlapping joint construction. 5.25 x 6" with a picture size of 2.75 x 3.5". Value $140-$165.

PAINTED WOOD, ca. 1840. American frame with mitered corners, an ogee middle area, and a painted finish of old green paint. 14.75 x 18.5" with a picture size of 10 x 14". Value $200-$300.

PAINTED WOOD, ca. 1840. An American frame with simple mitered corners, a second planed surface at the outside edge makes it a better frame. The painted finish is made to resemble exotic wood. 13.25 x 17.25" with a picture size of 10 x 14". Value $350-$450.

PAINTED WOOD, ca. 1840. American frame with mitered corners and a painted finish of crackled old brown paint. Folk art collectors desire the look of an old finish. 12.75 x 16.5" with a picture size of 10 x 14". Value $200-$300.

WOOD VENEER, ca. 1840. An American frame with overlapping joints and a mitered corner veneer of clear pine. The thick veneer is also applied to the outer sides giving a raised effect at the front edge. 11.25 x 13" with a picture size of 8 x 9.75". Value $200-$300.

PAINTED WOOD, ca. 1840. American frames with simple mitered corners and painted finishes made to resemble exotic woods. It is very difficult to find old painted frames in this popular size. 12.25-13.5 x 16.25-17.75" (outer dimensions vary) with a picture size of 10 x 14". Value $350-$450 each.

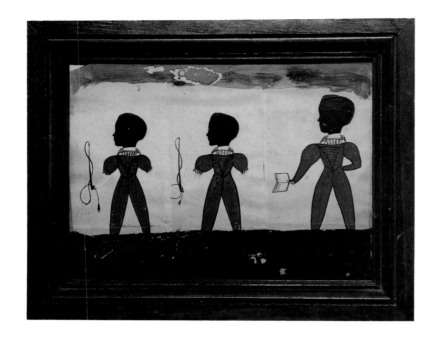

PAINTED WOOD, ca. 1840. An American frame with mitered corners and a painted finish made to resemble a grained wood. The varnish has darkened the finish over the past 150 years. 8.25 x 10.5" with a picture size of 7 x 9". Value $250-$325.

PAINTED WOOD, ca. 1840. An American frame with mitered corners and a painted finish using black, brown, and gold paint. 8.75 x 10" with a picture size of 8 x 9.5". Value $275-$350.

GILDED WOOD, ca. 1840. An American frame with an old patina gilded finish. The wear to the gilding should be left as is since it adds to the character of the frame. The sides are left unpainted as was common in those times to save money on the gilding expense. 6 x 7.25" with a picture size of 4.5 x 6". Value $150-$200.

PAINTED WOOD, ca. 1840. A small American frame with a gold paint on a clear wood pine. This was an inexpensive alternative to gilded frames at this time. The outer edges are unpainted. 6 x 7" with a picture size of 4 x 5". Value $100-$115.

PAINTED WOOD, ca. 1840. A small American frame with a complex moulding. It is painted black. 5.25 x 5.75" with a picture size of 2.75 x 3.25". Value $150-$175.

PAINTED WOOD, ca. 1840. An American frame with simple mitered corners and an excellent painted finish made to resemble tiger maple or tortoise. Difficult to find in this size. 14.75 x 16.75" with a picture size of 12 x 14". Value $500-$650.

RIPPLED WOOD, ca. 1840. An American frame with great ripple pattern and a painted finish that originally may have resembled wood. The finish has darkened. It is very difficult to find this style of frame. 16.25 x 19.75" with a picture size of 13.5 x 17". Value $600-$750.

PAINTED WOOD, ca. 1840. A small simple frame uses grooves and a bronze painted sight edge to bring the eye to the center of the frame. It is ideal for a portrait miniature. 7.25 x 8.75" with a picture size of 4 x 5". Value $150-$175.

GILDED, ca. 1845. A simple wooden frame with a gold leafed finish. 11.75 x 15.75" with a picture size of 10 x 13.75". The outside edge is not gilded. Value $200-$250.

PAINTED WOOD, ca. 1840. An American frame with mitered corners and a painted black finish with a gold painted sight edge. 15.25 x 18" with a picture size of 11.75 x 14". Value $300-$400.

BRASS SHELL ON WOOD, ca. 1845. A small American frame with a brass shell moulding. The brass shell is laid over the wooden moulding and crimped into the sides and tabbed into the back of the frame. 6 x 6.5" with a picture size of 5 x 5.5". Value $400-$450.

MAPLE AND MAHOGANY, ca. 1845. Maple and mahogany veneers make this handsome American frame perfect for a portrait miniature or a Daguerreotype. 7.25 x 7.75" with a picture size of 3.25 x 4.25". Value $225-$300.

BRASS SHELL ON WOOD, ca. 1845. Two small American frames with brass shell overlays. The brass shell is laid over the wooden moulding and crimped into the sides and tabbed into the back of the frame. 4.5 x 5" with a picture size of 3.25 x 3.5". Value $325-$375 each.

MAHOGANY, ca. 1845. Mahogany veneer with mitered corners on the front and an overlapped pine on the back. Usually used for portrait miniatures, silhouettes, or Daguerreotypes. 4.5 x 5.5" with a picture size of 3 x 4". Value $145-$175 each.

PAINTED WOOD, ca. 1850. An American frame with mitered corners and a painted floral design. Possibly from Pennsylvania. 7 x 9" with a picture size of 5 x 7". Value $275-$350.

MULTI PHOTOGRAPH, ca. 1850. This was made to hold four daguerreotypes. It has five levels of framing with gilt trim. The widest moulding is a veneered ogee burley walnut. The back shows the hand work and multiple layers. 14.5 x 16.5" with an overall picture size of 8 x 10". Each opening is 3.5 x 4.5". Value $400-$550.

MAHOGANY, 1850. This style and variations of this style can be found containing Currier & Ives or other period prints. The veneer is usually mahogany. Value depends on the quality of the wood and the complexity of the frame. 12.25 x 14.25" with a picture size of 8.5 x 10.5". Value $95-$175.

MAHOGANY, ca. 1850. A better mahogany veneer frame using a nicely grained wood. The back is also illustrated to show construction. 15.25 x 20.5" with a picture size of 9.25 x 14.5". Value $125-$175.

MAHOGANY, ca. 1850. This small elegant mahogany veneered frame likely held a daguerreotype or miniature painting. The back of the frame shows the three levels of construction. The center band is chamfered. 8.5 x 9.5" with a picture size of 3.5 x 4.5". Value $145-$175.

MAHOGANY, ca. 1850. A superb mahogany veneer frame that uses the finest grained wood. The back is also illustrated to show construction. 14 x 15.75" with a picture size of 7.5 x 9.25". Value $350-$450.

AMBROTYPE, ca. 1857. A quarter plate thermoplastic frame with period styling. 5.5 x 6.5". Value $185-$250.

AMBROTYPE, ca. 1857. Thermoplastic frame with birds. The frame is made of molded "Vulcanized" wood with the addition of hard rubber. 6.5 x 4". Value $95-$125.

WALNUT, ca. 1860. A nicely executed complex frame with porcelain buttons in the center of the corners. These white glass or china buttons were popular during the 1860s. 15 x 17" with a picture size of 8 x 10". Value $200-$250.

WALNUT OVAL, ca. 1860. A finely hand carved oval frame with a large crest at the bottom. May have been made in Pennsylvania. 13 x 18.5" with a picture size of 9 x 11". Value $250-$350.

VENEER, ca. 1860. An unusual simple dark veneered frame with a very open grain wood. 5.75 x 7.5" with a picture size of 4.125 x 5.75". Value $45-$60.

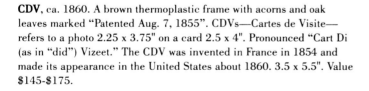

CDV, ca. 1860. A brown thermoplastic frame with acorns and oak leaves marked "Patented Aug. 7, 1855". CDVs—Cartes de Visite—refers to a photo 2.25 x 3.75" on a card 2.5 x 4". Pronounced "Cart Di (as in "did") Vizeet." The CDV was invented in France in 1854 and made its appearance in the United States about 1860. 3.5 x 5.5". Value $145-$175.

 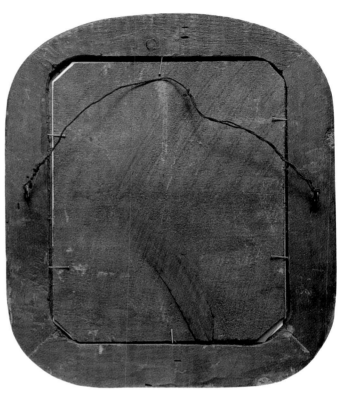

ROUNDED CORNER, ca. 1860. A two level walnut frame with a bronzed lip. The back view shows the original wooden slat that was used to back the picture. 11.5 x 13.25" with a picture size of 8 x 10". Value $200-$300.

WALNUT, 1860-1875. One of the most popular styles of frame that can be found on paintings and photographs of this period is the walnut frame. It is usually a complex frame of two or three layers, although single layers exist. It can be found with black, painted sections. The lip can be plain, painted, bronzed, gold leafed, or gold leafed with a pattern. A useful aspect of these frames is that they can be found in larger sizes, are sometimes reasonably priced, and can be cut down to fit any picture. Value $65-$250 depending upon size and embellishment.

CDV, ca. 1861. Thermoplastic frame with sunflowers. These thermoplastic frames were very fragile and often have damage to the edges. 3.5 x 5.25". Value $135-$175.

CDV, ca. 1864. A brown pressed paperboard made to resemble a thermoplastic frame. 4.5 x 7". To keep costs down, photo gallery owners needed to be able to provide a ready to hang portrait at very little cost. Value $35-$45.

TORTOISE, ca. 1865. An early style of tortoise marbling, done with a feather, on a complex frame with a gold leafed lip. This is a deep frame with the glass set in front of the inner moulding to give a shadow box effect. It is an especially striking frame. 10.5 x 14.75" with a picture size of 6.5 x 10.75". Value $450-$550.

PAINTED METAL, ca. 1865. A small metal oval with an unusual gesso and gold paint finish. 2.25 x 3.25" with a picture size of 2.5 x 3.5". Value $35-$50.

WALNUT AND TORTOISE, ca. 1868. An early style of tortoise marbling on a complex frame with a gold leafed lip. 12 x 13.75" with a picture size of 8 x 10". Value $200-$300.

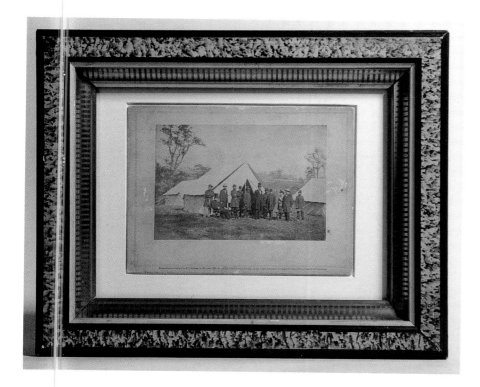

TORTOISE, ca. 1868. Tortoise marbling on a complex frame with a gold leafed lip. The gold leafed cove has been tinted to give the illusion that it is carved. This cove treatment was popular throughout the 1860s. It is very difficult to find good quality 1860s frames for pictures smaller than 8 x 10". 8.75 x 10.5" with a picture size of 6 x 8.75". Value $200-$300.

OVAL, ca. 1868. A small gold filled metal frame containing a painting on ivory of Abraham Lincoln. The painting was done by American artist Thomas Hicks (1823-1890), and the frame, contained in a leather bound, fitted velvet case, is contemporary with the painting. 2.66 x 4.33". Value $100-$150 with leather case.

CDV, ca. 1868. Cast iron frame. 3 x 5.75". Value $45-$60.

DECORATED GILDED COVE, ca. 1868. An interesting frame with a water gilded sight edge. The decorated gilded center moulding gives this frame a Florentine look. 13.25 x 16.75" with a picture size of 11 x 14". Value $150-$200.

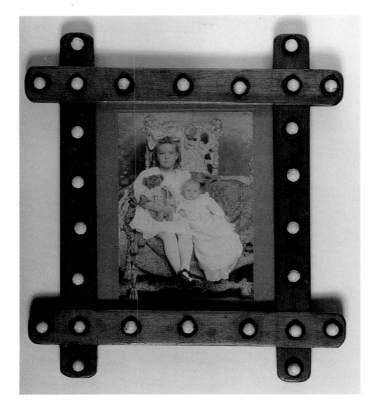

GLASS BEADED CRISS-CROSS, ca. 1870. This appears to be a homemade frame as the ends of each beam are hand finished and irregular. This type of glass or porcelain bead was a popular decoration from 1860 to 1870. 8.5 x 11.5" with a picture size of 5.5 x 6.5". Value $110-$145.

TRAMP ART, ca. 1870. A wonderful tramp art piece in wood. The frame is chip carved and is made from old cigar boxes. It has a superb patina and exhibits professional artistic qualities. These are actively sought by folk art collectors. 7.5 x 12" with a picture size of 4.5 x 6.5". Value $400-$500.

OVAL, ca. 1870. A delicate walnut frame. 10.25 x 13.5" with a picture size of 9 x 12". Value $100-$150.

CARVED WALNUT, ca. 1870. A finely carved frame in the shape of branches gives this a refined but natural look. 12 x 14" with a picture size of 8 x 10". Value $250-$350.

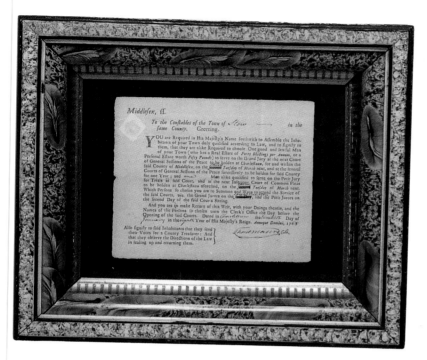

TORTOISE, ca. 1870. A two color tortoise marbling in a complex frame with a gold leafed lip. The gilded inner moulding has been decorated to give the illusion that it is carved. 12 x 14" with a picture size of 8 x 10". Value $200-$250.

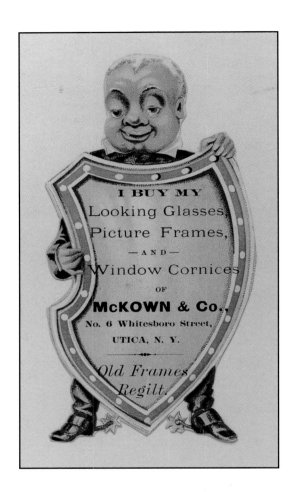

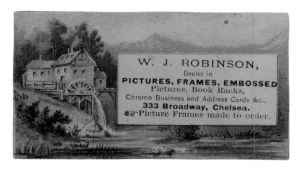

~A.~ CLARKE,~

Manufacturer of

Picture Frames & Mouldings

OF ALL DESCRIPTIONS,

Importer of French Plate Glass,

Office and Salesroom : 788 South Second Street,

PHILADELPHIA.

BUSINESS CARDS, ca. 1870. Two business cards for picture framers.

F. W. HERRICK,

——DEALER IN——

PICTURE FRAMES,

WINDOW CORNICES,

CHROMOS, LOOKING GLASSES, ETC., ETC.,

WARRENSBURGH, N. Y.

Small Pictures ENLARGED a Specialty.

TORTOISE, ca. 1870. A small tortoise marbled frame of two layers with a silver leafed lip. 8.75 x 10.5" with a picture size of 8.75 x 10.5". Value $150-$200.

EASTLAKE STYLE, ca. 1872. A black lacquer finish with an incised, delicate pattern. The oil gilded outer edge and sight edge show the frame maker's inability to let go of the traditional finish on the new Eastlake style. 9.5 x 11.5" with a picture size of 8 x 10". Value $100-$150.

OVAL, ca. 1870. A very warm gilded surface on an oval walnut frame. 11 x 12.75" with a picture size of 9 x 10.75". Value $100-$125.

WALNUT, ca. 1875. A popular style of frame with added leaf shaped corners and some reeding on the outer moulding. 11.25 x 13.25" with a picture size of 8 x 10". Value $75-$100.

MAHOGANY, ca. 1875. An American mahogany frame with crisscross corners and a small raised wooden diamonds. 11.5 x 13.25" with a picture size of 8 x 10". Value $95-$125.

WALNUT, ca. 1875. At first this appears to be the standard style walnut frame, but the finely carved and incised outer moulding makes it a better frame. 12.75 x 14.75" with a picture size of 8 x 10". Value $200-$250.

Above:
EASTLAKE STYLE, ca. 1875. The Eastlake style is usually characterized by a dark lacquer finish with an incised, delicate pattern. The mat is original to the frame and shows the same style of delicate lines. 9.25 x 13.5" with a picture size of 7.75 x 9.75". Value $200-$250.

EASTLAKE STYLE, ca. 1875. The tortoise shell finish with an incised, delicate pattern. The sides of the frame are unfinished, indicating that this may have been an inner moulding for a larger frame. 11.5 x 13.5" with a picture size of 8 x 10. Value $75-$100.

EASTLAKE STYLE, ca. 1875. A painted burl wood finish with an incised, delicate pattern. The outer edge is gilded as is the sight edge. 12.75 x 14.5" with a picture size of 8 x 10". Value $175-$200.

EASTLAKE STYLE, ca. 1875. This is a very fine frame that combines three complex layers to make one eye-catching design. The outer layer is oak with black incised line trim. The center moulding is silver leafed with a golden orange shellac finish and a repeating pattern. The inner moulding is an incised design on a black lacquer finish (the typical Eastlake style embellishment). 14.25 x 16.25" with a picture size of 8 x 10". Value $300-$400.

OAK, ca. 1875. A two level oak frame with applied compo design in the center moulding. The rope twist inner moulding may have originally been silver leafed. 12.5 x 14.25" with a picture size of 8 x 10". Value $145-$175.

EASTLAKE STYLE, ca. 1879. More commonly, Eastlake style frames were made with incised lines on a lacquered surface. However, furniture in the Eastlake style was characterized by wood turnings and balls on rods. This almost folk art style frame uses some of these furniture elements to add character without distracting from the picture within the frame. 10.25 x 13" with a picture size of 7 x 10". Value $250-$300.

TRAMP ART, ca. 1875. A polychrome tramp art piece in wood. The frame is chip carved. It is unusual to find multi-colored frames in this style. 15 x 23.5" with a picture size of 11.25 x 19". Value $500-$600.

OAK, ca. 1880. A simple wooden frame with a black incised moulding. The mat is contemporary with the frame. 9.5 x 11.5" with a picture size of 8 x 10". Value $150-$200.

TORTOISE FINISH, ca. 1880. A complex frame of three levels with the glass in front of the sight moulding. This type of tortoise finish was popular from 1870 to about 1885. 10 x 12" with a picture size of 6.5 x 8.5. The frame is 2.25" deep. Value $125-$200.

GILDED, ca. 1880. A finely made, high relief oak leaves and acorns design in a three part complex frame. 13.75 x 16.25" with a picture size of 9.75 x 12.5". Value $350-$500.

PINE CONE, ca. 1880. A rustic or Adirondack style frame. The rustic look was popularized In the Adirondack mountains of New York. A style emerged that would fit in with the elegant, rustic cabins that many wealthy New Yorkers were building. Many examples can be found, from the simple to the complex. Deceptively simple, the pine cones were glued and sewn into place. 6.25 x 7.25" with a picture size of 2.5 x 4.5". Value $55-$75.

PINE CONE, ca. 1880. A rustic or Adirondack style frame. This example is beautifully made and probably would have hung vertically rather than horizontally. 12.75 x 14.25" with a picture size of 8 x 10". Value $125-$225.

FOLK ART WALNUT, ca. 1880. A handsomely made walnut faced frame that appears to be made with pieces of other frames. The back shows a complex construction. Rather than use plain mitered ends, the maker cut strange zig zag mitered ends that fit into each other. This is very time consuming hand labor that appears to have been done just for the pleasure of doing it rather than for structural integrity. 14.75 x 16.5" with a picture size of 8 x 9.75". Value $275-$325.

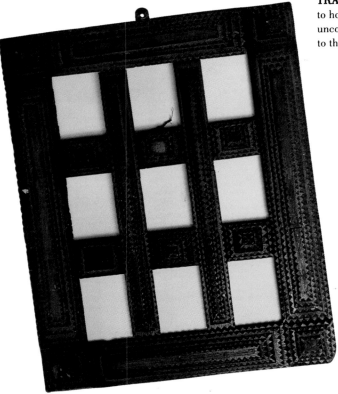

TRAMP ART, ca. 1880. A chip carved Tramp art wooden frame made to hold a group of CDVs or similar small photographs. It is an uncomplicated chip carved pattern but has more value and appeal due to the format of nine photos. 15 x 19". Value $275-$325.

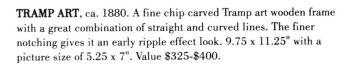

TRAMP ART, ca. 1880. A fine chip carved Tramp art wooden frame with a great combination of straight and curved lines. The finer notching gives it an early ripple effect look. 9.75 x 11.25" with a picture size of 5.25 x 7". Value $325-$400.

GILDED, ca. 1880. A high relief floral design frame with fine details. 13.5 x 17.25" with a picture size of 9.5 x 13.25". Value $350-$450.

OAK, ca. 1880. A hand painted two level oak frame. The mat for the photo is a page from a Victorian cabinet card album. 12 x 14.25" with a picture size of 8 x 10". Value $115-$135.

OAK, ca. 1880. The pearls laid into the center moulding and the effect obtained by leaving the sight edge uncut at the corners gives this simple oak frame a touch of elegance. 12.5 x 15" with a picture size of 10 x 12.5". Value $200-$250.

HEAVY COMPO, ca. 1880. A compo covered frame with four levels in a very dark finish. The site edge has a scalloped shell pattern. The next level is a brown or rust colored velvet. The outer center band is a bundled sheaf of twigs and outside edge is a repeating leaf pattern. The quality of each level is very high. This busy Victoriana yields a very heavy looking frame. 20 x 22". Value $200-$250.

VICTORIAN HEAVY COMPO, ca. 1880. A gilded finish on a busy Natural motif pattern. Leaves, flowers, and a basket weave are combined in this Aesthetic style frame. The maker used bronze and gilded finishes. These heavily covered frames are often found with chunks of the surface missing. With a repeating pattern, they can sometimes be repaired. 13 x 15" with a picture size of 8 x 10". Value $175-$225.

HEAVY COMPO, ca. 1885. This example of a high relief floral design frame exhibits very nice qualities. A frame with this much activity would compete with and could overwhelm the picture within it. 14.25 x 16.25". Value $200-$250.

RAILROAD STYLE, ca. 1880. The frame gets its name due its similarity to a set of railroad tracks. It is a combination of oak center bands, a clearer wood, perhaps pine for the turned and split outer band, and composition on wood for the site edge and top and bottom outer edges. 6.75 x 13" with a picture size of 4.25 x 6". Value $135-$175.

OAK, ca. 1885. A two level oak frame with applied compo design in the center moulding. This is an exceptional quality example. 15 x 20" with a picture size of 11 x 16". Value $200-$300.

OAK, ca. 1885. A two level oak frame with applied compo design in the inner and outer mouldings. 18.5 x 23.5" with a picture size of 16 x 20". Value $150-$200.

FAUX OAK WOOD, ca. 1885. A pine frame with a machine applied painted oak grain. A clue to the faux finish is that there is no indentation where the grain marks are and a fingernail pushed into the wood will make an indentation. Old oak is generally too hard to indent with a fingernail. 18.25 x 22.75" with a picture size of 16 x 20". Value $85-$100.

GILDED, ca. 1885. This example of a low relief floral design compo covered frame exhibits very nice qualities. The lack of finish on the outside edge indicates that this could be the inner moulding of a larger frame. 11 x 13" with a picture size of 8 x 10". Value $75-$100.

OAK PANEL, ca. 1885. An oak panel frame. The panels are basically flat but a have raised rim. 11 x 13" with a picture size of 7.5 x 9.5". Value $100-$140.

CABINET CARD, ca. 1885. A child stands next to a large portrait of her dad, the fire captain. The portrait sits on an easel that was typical in many Victorian homes. While the frame in the photo is fairly attractive and certainly looks good on the painting, it would be difficult to use in a modern day home. There are many lesser quality ornate Victorian frames that show up at country auctions or in antique shops that are better left where they are found.

COMPO, ca. 1890. Two examples of inexpensive heavy compo frames. These were turned out by the thousands for the average person who wanted an inexpensive fancy frame. Some of the points that distinguish these from higher quality frames are the bronze powder finish on all parts, the single level of moulding rather than an added lip (simple vs. complex), the poor quality of the attachment of the compo to the frame (gaps) and from the rear, the holes are simply drilled through the frame rather than showing any sign of carving. The closer you look, the worse it looks. Value $75-$125.

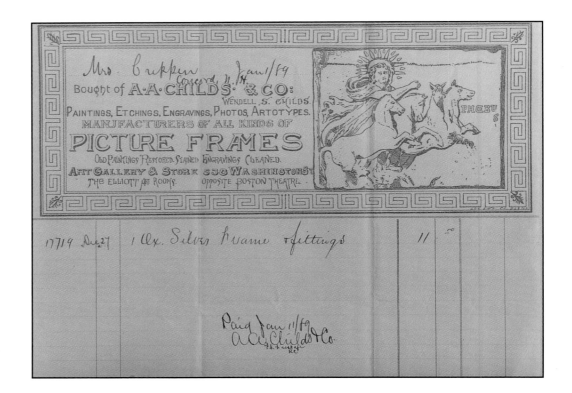

BILLHEAD, 1889. A bill for a dozen silver frame fittings from A.A. Childs & Co.

TRAMP ART, ca. 1890. A finer example of a chip carved Tramp art wooden frame. It shows an unmeasured group of curves, obviously made without a pattern. It has a lot of character. 8.5 x 11" with a picture size of 4.25 x 6.25". Value $325-$375.

FOLK ART, ca. 1890. A beautiful frame made of mahogany and pine hand carved woods. Each corner still bears the shadow of a star. 12.25 x 14.5" with a picture size of 7.25 x 9.25". Value $550-$650.

FOLK ART, ca. 1890. A pretty frame made of a mahogany stained oak. Each piece was hand carved and set to create a pleasing but not distracting pattern that leads your eye to the picture area. The frame is built as a shadow box with approximately .5" of depth. 10.5 x 12.5" with a picture size of 7 x 9". Value $450-$550.

VICTORIAN, ca. 1890. Typical of the Victorian period frames is the velvet center band. This also has a gilded sight edge with its string of pearls design. The outside edges are a floral leaf and fruit or bell flower design in composition that has been toned with gilded highlights. 9.5 x 11.5" with a picture size of 4.25 x 6". Two things that add value are the modest size of the frame and the tasteful blending of all the elements. Value $135-$175.

ADVERTISING FRAME, ca. 1890. An ad for A.C. Yates Clothing with Palmer Cox Brownies holding up the banner is framed by a compo covered simple "D" shaped frame. The design is leaves and trellises with strings of graduated pearls. 12 x 12". Value with the advertising $650-$800.

OAK, ca. 1895. A simple oak frame with no ornamentation other than grooves. It did not compete with whatever it surrounded. 16.5 x 19.5" with a picture size of 14 x 17". Value $50-$90.

SORRENTO, ca. 1890. This is a very elaborate frame. To make it, the artisan had to draw the design, drill numerous holes, and then use a scroll saw to cut out each shape. This scroll cut style is called Sorrento. Sorrento became popular at the 1876 Centennial and lasted into the 1900s. The lettering, curves, and applied gilt to the picture openings make this an exceptional frame. 13 x 15". Value $350-$425.

STAMPED DESIGN, ca. 1895. A oak frame with a gilded sight edge and stamped designs centered in each side of the center moulding. 11.25 x 13.25" with a picture size of 8 x 10". Value $150-$175.

FRENCH STYLE, ca. 1895. The ribbon detail at the top of this simple frame is called a French ribbon. 9 x 10.5". Value $145-$200.

PYROGRAPHY, ca. 1895. The design on this wooden frame was made by drawing with a hot soldering iron-like device. This is a particularly elegant frame due to the excellent execution of the Gibson Girl and the shading of the background. 7.75 x 10" with a picture size of 4 x 5.5". Value $175-$225.

PALMER COX, ca. 1898. A simple wooden frame with applied paper strips of Palmer Cox's Brownies. The frame holds an autographed drawing of one of the Brownies. 5 x 6" with a picture size of 3.25 x 4.5". Value $250-$275.

TRAMP ART, ca. 1900. A small tramp art wooden frame using a repeating heart design. This is a very nice example of a better quality piece. The wood was first carved into curves and then decorated by chip carving. 4.25 x 5.5" with a picture size of 2.5 x 3.75". Value $120-$155.

TRAMP ART, ca. 1900. A standard example of a chip carved Tramp art wooden frame made from an old cigar box. 6.75 x 8.75" with a picture size of 4.75 x 6.5". Value $110-$145.

TRAMP ART, ca. 1900. A chip carved Tramp art wooden frame in the shape of a five sided star. It shows a measured group of cuts, obviously made with a pattern. 10.5" from point to farthest point. Value $225-$275.

FRAME FINISHING SHOP, ca. 1900. An unknown frame gilder's work room. As there are no saws, straight mouldings, or vises visible in the photo, it is likely that whoever used this room just worked on finishes for frames.

SEA SHELLS, ca. 1900. These attractive frames were probably sold as souvenirs at Atlantic City or some other beach resort area. The shells are glued onto a paper board material and each has a hanger and easel back for wall or tabletop use. 5.5 x 8". Value $60-$80 each.

GILDED COMPO, ca. 1901. A superb, high relief compo frame made to compliment the painting of lower Manhattan by Charles Appel. The frame is original to this 1901 painting. 20.25 x 26.25" with a picture size of 12 x 18". Value $1,500-$2,000.

FRENCH CURVES, ca. 1905. A French made frame with applied gesso decoration, gilded highlights and edges, a row of beads near the sight edge, and a soft curve to the sides and corners. 8.5 x 10.5" with a picture size of 7 x 9". Value $95-$125.

FRENCH CURVES, ca. 1905. A French made frame with applied gesso decoration, gilded highlights and edges, and a soft curve to the sides and corners. 18.5 x 22.5" with a picture size of 16 x 19.5".
Value $175-$250.

ICONOGRAPHIC, ca. 1905. This frame is representative of a series of frames that have painted compo images applied to the simple dark oak frame. The images reinforce the picture in the frame and the two should generally be left together. Themes that you may find include: the drinkers, the smokers, babies, golfers, football players, romance, etc. This example has a very popular cowboy theme which makes it more valuable. 18 x 33". Value with cowboy image $250-$350, value with other images $75-$200.

ARTS AND CRAFTS, ca. 1905. A simple oak frame with a copper button at the corners. Unusual in that its side pieces are beveled. 13.5 x 20" with a picture size of 10 x 17". Value without the picture $75-$90.

ART NOUVEAU, ca. 1910. A superb gold leafed, hand carved wood frame from the workshop of Frederick Loeser & Co., Brooklyn, New York. Signed frames by known and desirable makers add a premium to the frame's value. Loeser's work is actively sought. 15 x 19" with a picture size of 11 x 13.75". Value $4,000 -$6,000.

RIGHT ANGLE EXTENSION, ca. 1910. The right angle extensions design was originally introduced in Southern Germany in the early 17th century. The original 17th century frame would have been hand carved wood rather than compo covered wood. 14.75 x 17.5" with a picture size of 11 x 13.5. Value $200-$300.

HANDCRAFTED, ca. 1910. A beautiful small frame with an ecclesiastic look. This frame has attributes similar to those found on frames made by Charles Pendergast and Frederick Harer—the incised designs are hand colored, gilded, and decorated with punch work. 10.5 x 12.5" with a picture size of 8 x 10. Value $150-$200.

WALNUT PANEL, ca. 1910. A elegant polished American walnut frame. The panels are basically flat but have the nice touch of a raised rim and a cove cut sight edge. This photo does not show the highly polished surface of the wood. 11.5 x 13.75" with a picture size of 6.5 x 9". Value $200-$300.

OAK, ca. 1915. A simple oak, mitered corner frame. 12 x 14.75" with a picture size of 10 x 13". Value $100-$135.

OAK, ca. 1915. A simple oak frame with applied cast iron corners. 17 x 20" with a picture size of 11 x 14". Value $65-$85.

HOMESPUN, ca. 1915. This frame was made by wrapping thread over an eight sided form and adding material to finish it. This was a home craft that became popular during the first World War. The size is 4 x 6". Value $45-$55.

HOMESPUN, ca. 1915. Another homespun frame made by wrapping thread over a form. The pattern of the thread gives this a strange ink-blot look. The size is 4 x 6". Value $45-$55.

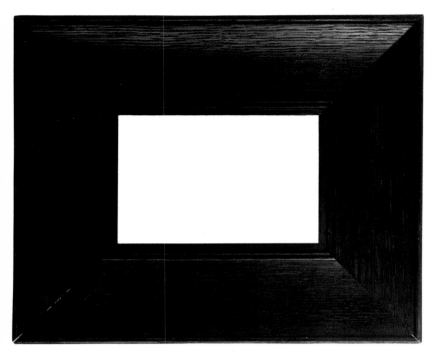

MISSION OAK, ca. 1918. A simple dark oak frame with detail at the sight edge and the outer edge. 8.25 x 10" with a picture size of 3.75 x 5.5". Value $100-$135.

FABRIC, ca. 1920. An unusual lace and lamé covered paperboard frame with a delicate rosette oval. 7 x 8.75" with a picture size of 4 x 5.75". Value $45-$60.

MATCH STICK ART, ca. 1920. Match stick frames may have originated in prisons. Prisoners would assemble match sticks into whimsical and useful small items. Prisons with prison stores sold convict made items. Obviously, if prisoners could make these, anyone with some patience and a supply of used match sticks could too. These are now considered to be a form of folk art. This is a nice quality piece. The value range covers all match stick frames. 7 x 12". Value $75-$300.

MAHOGANY, ca. 1920. A good quality polished wood frame that can be used with most prints or photographs. These are the types of frames that you should not pass up when they are offered reasonably. This piece has some character and is very usable. 15 x 18.5" with a picture size of 10.5 x 14". Value $60-$85.

ART DECO WOOD, ca. 1928. A small Deco frame with black inset corners. 3.625 x 4.625" with a picture size of 3.375 x 4.375". Value $60-$80.

ART DECO WOOD, ca. 1929. A bronze powder finish gives a soft gold touch to this style of frame popular in the mid-1920 to early 1930s. Made in England and sold by the Victoria & Albert Museum gift shop. The center groove is painted green. 7.5 x 9" with a picture size of 6.75 x 8.5". Value $45-$75.

ROARING '20s, ca. 1928. Simple grooved lines on a rounded gesso covered frame with finished corners give this frame an elegant feel. It works well with the nude contained therein. The size is 12.5 x 15.5" with a picture size of 11 x 14". Value $65-$80.

ART DECO WOOD, ca. 1929. Bronze powder adds a muted gold touch to this style of frame that was popular in the mid-1920 to early 1930s. 13.5 x 16.5" with a picture size of 11 x 14". Value $85-$125.

Table Top Frames

DAGUERREOTYPE, ca. 1843. An early Daguerreotype case made by William Shew, showing a bird at the fountain design on the front and a Moorish or Islamic design on the back. The Islamic design element reappeared in the 1880s on wall frames. 3.5 x 3.75". Value $75-$125.

DAGUERREOTYPE, ca. 1845. Early Daguerreotypes had a simple pebble finished mat. This mat style was made from the early 1840s to the mid-1840s. Both have later preservers.

DAGUERREOTYPE, ca. 1843. The earliest Daguerreotypes have a simple pebble finished mat and were not held in a preserver. This mat style was made from the early 1840s to the mid-1840s. William Shew invented this type of case in 1843. The earliest cases had a plain silk cushion and the decoration of the outside of the case was simple. 3.5 x 3.75".

DAGUERREOTYPE, ca. 1847. During the first ten years of the Daguerreotype, the mat had a simple pebble finish and there was no preserver. This mat style was made from the late 1840s to the early 1850s. 3.5 x 3.75".

DAGUERREOTYPE, ca. 1857. Thermoplastic Daguerreotype cases—The Piano Lesson (by A. Schaefer) and Cupid & Stag, made by Littlefield, Parsons & Co. These are sixth plate cases, 2.5 x 3". Value $125-$150.

DAGUERREOTYPE, ca. 1857. Thermoplastic Daguerreotype case. One of the two larger makers was Littlefield, Parsons & Co. The mat is decorated with shells and curlicues. 3.5 x 3.75".

DAGUERREOTYPE, ca. 1857. Thermoplastic Daguerreotype case with Dag. One of the two larger case makers was A. P. Crichlow & Co. The mat is decorated with thistles and vines and held in a preserver. 3.5 x 3.75".

DAGUERREOTYPES, ca. 1857. These mat styles were made from the late 1850s to the 1860s. They do not have the pebble finish and the preserver is appropriate.

DAGUERREOTYPE, ca. 1857. Thermoplastic daguerreotype or ambrotype cases. Value $125-$150.

DAGUERREOTYPE, ca. 1858. A later Daguerreotype with a beautiful mat and simple preserver. This mat style was made from the mid-1850s to about 1860. 3.5 x 3.75".

AMBROTYPE, ca. 1858. In this typical cased ambrotype, the thermoplastic case holds a blue velvet cushion and the ambrotype is framed by a scalloped oval mat. The preserver has embellishments at the corners and center points. 2.5 x 3".

AMBROTYPE, ca. 1859. Another example of a cased ambrotype. The ambrotype is framed by a decorated oval mat. The preserver has embellishments at the corners and center points. 3.5 x 3.75".

AMBROTYPES, ca. 1859. Examples of cased ambrotypes. Many mat styles were available to the customer. Frontier photographers tended to use a simpler style of mat and preserver. These mat styles were made from the late 1850s to the 1860s.

PATRIOTIC MAT, ca. 1861. This rare mat has a Civil War patriotic theme. It shows the nation's flag, ship, and a cannon and the words "Constitution and Union." Quarter plate size.

AMBROTYPE, ca. 1862. Another example of a cased ambrotype. The soldier is framed by a decorated round corner mat. The preserver has embellishments at the corners and center points. 2.5 x 3".

AMBROTYPE CASE, ca. 1862. Thermoplastic case with a patriotic motif and slogan. Value $125-$175.

MAT, GLASS, AND PRESERVER, ca. 1863. This shows the parts of a typical period photograph. The photograph was held in a sandwich of cover glass, then a decorative brass mat, then the ambrotype or daguerreotype, all held in a "preserver" of thin copper or brass wrap-a-round frame.

WIRE, ca. 1870. A small wire and glass frame made to hold a Carte de Visite photograph. The back is also illustrated to show construction. 2.75 x 4". Value $60-$75.

PIETRA DURA, ca. 1870. Pietra dura is a decorating process of stone inlaid with stone. Generally made in Italy, it was popular from the 1850s (broaches and earrings can be found in this style) to the 1870s. The stone is set into the cover of this hinged brass frame. 6.75 x 7.75" with a picture size of 5.5 x 6.5". *Courtesy of P.H.P. Hall Of Frames*, Value $700-$800.

SWIVEL STAND, ca. 1880. A very nice brass swinging easel frame with beveled glass. 6.25 x 8.5" with a picture size of 4.25 x 6.5", a cabinet card size. *Courtesy of P.H.P. Hall Of Frames*, Value $250-$300.

EASTLAKE STYLE, ca. 1872. A black lacquer finish with an incised, delicate pattern and a wire easel back. 7.5 x 12" with a picture size of 6 x 8". Value $100-$150.

STERLING SILVER, ca. 1880. Sterling silver frames were a mainstay in Victorian homes. These two examples are English made and are hallmarked. (L-R) 6 x 7", 6.75 x 10". *Courtesy of P.H.P. Hall Of Frames*, Value (L-R) $400-$450, $400-$475.

BOOK STYLE, ca. 1880. A highly raised pattern brass frame with a cover. 5.5 x 7.5" with a picture size of 4.25 x 6.5", a cabinet card size. *Courtesy of P.H.P. Hall Of Frames*, Value $350-$425.

BRASS HALF, ca. 1880. An French cabinet card frame with hand set stones and a small inset watercolor at the bottom. 5 x 7". Value $275-$300.

BRASS, ca. 1880. An French cabinet card frame with painted highlights. 5 x 7". Value $275-$300.

BRASS, ca. 1880. A French cabinet card frame with flowers along a fence. 5 x 7". Value $275-$300.

BRASS HORIZONTAL, ca. 1880. A wonderful cast brass easel frame in a hard to find horizontal format, obviously made for a photo of two or three people. 5.5 x 8". Value $150-$175.

ENGLISH BRASS, ca. 1885. This good looking frame combines a simple frame with a decorative surround. 4.5 x 7" with a picture size of 2.5 x 4". *Courtesy of P.H.P. Hall Of Frames*, Value $275-$325.

HAND ENAMELED BRASS, ca. 1885. A beautiful, hand enameled brass European frame 5 x 6.5" with a picture size of 4 x 5.5". *Courtesy of P.H.P. Hall Of Frames*, Value $225-$275.

MIRROR, ca. 1885. A brass triple mirror marked "Wagon Fork, NY" that could stand on a table top or be hung on a wall. 8.5 x 10.5" closed. *Courtesy of P.H.P. Hall Of Frames*, Value $175-$225.

BRASS, ca. 1888. A brass frame with lots of detail. 5.25 x 8.25". *Courtesy of P.H.P. Hall Of Frames*, Value $225-$275.

GILDED BRASS, ca. 1890. A substantial table top frame made to hold an oval portrait. It has sort of a busy Art Nouveau style. 10 x 14.25" with a picture size of 5.75 x 7.75". *Courtesy of P.H.P. Hall Of Frames,* Value $200-$300.

GILDED BRASS, ca. 1890. A substantial table top frame made to hold an oval portrait. The back shows the tabs used to keep the photo in place and the pivoting leg that allows the frame to stand up. 10.25 x 13.5" with a picture size of 5.75 x 7.75". Value $100-$150.

GILDED BRASS, ca. 1890. A table top frame with dragons in the design. 10 x 14.25" with a picture size of 5.25 x 6.5". *Courtesy of P.H.P. Hall Of Frames*, Value $200-$300.

FLORAL, ca. 1890. Small flowers create the framing. 4.5 x 4.75". *Courtesy of P.H.P. Hall Of Frames*, Value $100-$170 .

STERLING SILVER, ca. 1890. These are English made and are hall-marked. The frame on the left is a traditional wall frame style. The one on the right has a gold wash and a wood back. (L-R) 7 x 9", 5 x 7.25". *Courtesy of P.H.P. Hall Of Frames*, Value (L-R) $300-$400, $300-$400.

BRONZE, ca. 1890. A cast bronze frame with open lace work corners. 2.25 x 2.75". *Courtesy of P.H.P. Hall Of Frames*, Value $125-$175 .

MIRROR, ca. 1890. A Brass triple frame with celluloid covered prints on the rear. The use of sheet celluloid as a covering for paper prints became very popular at the end of the 1880s. The mirror is shown with the flaps closed and open. It was designed to stand on a table or be hung on the wall. Closed, it is 11 x 12.5". *Courtesy of P.H.P. Hall Of Frames*, Value $250-$300.

ALUMINUM, ca. 1890. An English cast and engraved aluminum (spelled "aluminium" in England) cabinet card frame. When aluminum was first introduced, it was about as expensive as gold. When the smelting process was perfected, the price dropped dramatically. 5.5 x 7.5". Value $45-$60.

MOTHER-OF-PEARL, ca. 1890. An English cabinet card frame in mother-of-pearl and abalone. 4.5 x 7". Value $150-$175.

MASONIC, ca. 1890. A piece worn by a Free Mason of silver with rhinestones. It has been converted into an easel frame. Supposedly, upon the death of the Masonic member, the piece was to be returned to the lodge. 3 x 3.5". Value $100-$125.

MOTHER-OF-PEARL, ca. 1890. An English cabinet card frame in mother-of-pearl. 5 x 7". Value $150-$175.

BRASS ORIENTAL, ca. 1890. A nice cast brass frame with an Oriental motif. 6.5 x 8". Value $150-$175.

CARVED MARBLE, ca. 1890. A double photo frame in marble with a Moorish motif. 6.5 x 8". Value $150-$175.

LEAVES AND HAMMERED COPPER, ca. 1890. A busy frame of copper and wrought iron. 16 x 18". *Courtesy of P.H.P. Hall Of Frames,* Value $225-$275.

THREE METALS, ca. 1890. A beautiful English easel back frame in brass, silver, and copper. 8 x 10". Value $600-$700.

TRAVEL FRAME, ca. 1890. A tiny red leather covered wooden frame to hold two photos of loved ones. It folds up like a traveling alarm clock and could be put by the side of the bed by a traveling salesman or such. The size is 1 x 3". Value $55-$65.

TRAMP ART, ca. 1890. A "crown of thorns" style tramp art frame for two 5 x 7 inch photographs. This style of wood decoration is called "chip" or "notch" carving. The maker used a short knife and cut chips out of the wood. The wood used was often recycled from old cigar boxes or moulding strips. Crown of thorn items were made of interlocking pieces of wood. The name came from the crown of thorns that Jesus allegedly wore. 14" tall. Value $75-$100.

HIGH LEAD CAST TIN, ca. 1895. An unusual frame. Its front is a cast soft tin soldered to a sheet tin back and easel. This was an attempt to cut costs and produce good looking frames out of inexpensive materials. 5.25 x 8" with a picture size of 4.25 x 6". Value $50-$60.

THREE BRASS, ca. 1910, 1895, and 1895. The three frames are of substantial brass construction. The first is a wall frame style, the second is an Art Nouveau style and the third shows a Rococo style. 5.75 x 7", 5.25 x 7.5" and 6 x 8". *Courtesy of P.H.P. Hall Of Frames*, Value $250-$300 each.

PHOTO ALBUM, ca. 1896. An unusual cabinet card album/writing desk combination. Throughout the 19th and 20th centuries, mankind has tried to combine two things into one. Very often, as the case here, the idea does not suit both needs adequately. The decorative photo album opens to serve as a desk and store writing supplies. It was not a very good desk and it was an awkward photo album. *Courtesy of P.H.P. Hall Of Frames*, Value $95-$150.

SILVERPLATE, ca. 1900. A basket of fruit appears at the top and fruit and vines adorn the sides. 10 x 14". *Courtesy of P.H.P. Hall Of Frames*, Value $225-$275.

INLAID, ca. 1900. An English frame with a floral pattern inlaid into wood. It is often called "feather and pen" work. This was made to hold a cabinet card. 6.75 x 11.75" with a picture size of 4.25 x 6.5". *Courtesy of P.H.P. Hall Of Frames*, Value $300-$350.

GATE, ca. 1900. A popular Victorian theme was the image of the gate. It signified remembrance of those who passed on. This example is superb in that the gate is very detailed and includes a small working latch. It is shown open and closed. Made in England. 5.5 x 6.5". Value $600-$650.

BRASS, ca. 1900. The oval frame on the left is a French style. The general design is fairly common and can be found with many variations. The frame on the right is a beauty with a filigree effect. (L-R) 4.5 x 6.5", 6 x 6.75". *Courtesy of P.H.P. Hall Of Frames*, Value (L-R) $100-$145, $200-$275.

BRASS, ca. 1900. An oval solid brass frame with cherubs at the base. 7 x 11.25". *Courtesy of P.H.P. Hall Of Frames*, Value $275-$350.

BRASS, ca. 1900. The frame on the left is brass and is a beauty. The frame on the right has a filigreed look and was made from about 1900 to 1920. (L-R) 6.25 x 11", 6.5 x 9". *Courtesy of P.H.P. Hall Of Frames*, Value (L-R) $250-$300, $175-$225.

BRASS, ca. 1900. Two French, well made frames. The right frame is valued at about the same price as the more ornate frame on the left because it has domed glass. (L-R) 4.75 x 7" and 4 x 5". *Courtesy of P.H.P. Hall Of Frames*, Value $200-$275 each.

CAST BRASS, ca. 1900. An attractive heavy brass frame surrounding a hand painted portrait on porcelain. The center part of the frame is fabric with a handmade needlepoint design. These French porcelain portraits are usually found with their original frames and have become quite popular. 5.5 x 7". Value (portrait and frame) $550-$750.

CAST BRASS, ca. 1900. A French porcelain hand painted portrait with its original frame. The back side is also shown to show the combination stand, wall hanger, and brass tabs to hold the picture in place. 5 x 6.5". Value (portrait and frame) $550-$750.

CAST BRASS, ca. 1900. A French porcelain hand painted portrait and frame with cherubs. 7 x 8.5". Value (portrait and frame) $650-$850.

INLAID WOOD, ca. 1900. An Italian made frame with fine wood inlays. 4 x 7". Value $100-$150.

PERSIAN, ca. 1900. A double frame made in the middle east, probably Persia, of carved wood with mother-of-pearl and Ebony inlays. Each side is 10 x 15". Value $375-$425.

BURRWOOD, ca. 1900. A French made burrwood frame. 6 x 9". Value $100-$150.

ART NOUVEAU, ca. 1901. A very attractive pair of hammered and shaped gold plated wire frames with applied leaves. They are probably English. The fact that they were found as a pair adds to their desirability. 8 x 9" with a picture size of 4.25 x 6.25". Value $450-$550 for the pair.

ART NOUVEAU, ca. 1901. A beautiful cast bronze frame with a great combination of straight and curved lines. It has a swing arm stand on the back. The delicate highlighting of the center of the flowers adds to the frame's appeal. 8.5 x 11". Value $325-$400.

ART NOUVEAU BRONZE, ca. 1901. An ornate French bronze frame by Louchet. 6.5 x 9". Value $1,200-$1,350. *Courtesy of John Jesse Antiques.*

ART NOUVEAU, ca. 1901. A very pretty Art Nouveau influenced frame. The typical Nouveau style is elongated with delicate swirls. This brass frame is not elongated and the swirls are more densely packed. 5.25 x 6.5". *Courtesy of P.H.P. Hall Of Frames*, Value $250-$300.

HUTTON & SONS, ca. 1904. A fine silver and hand enameled frame designed by Hutton & Sons. 7 x 7". Value $2,700-$3,000. *Courtesy of John Jesse Antiques.*

ART NOUVEAU, ca. 1901. A brass and copper plated cast iron frame with soft curves. 8.5 x 10.5". *Courtesy of P.H.P. Hall Of Frames*, Value $350-$400.

ART NOUVEAU, ca. 1905. European oak with a copper trim showing the soft lines so popular with the Art Nouveau style. This was designed to hold a cabinet card. 9 x 9.5" with a picture size of 4.25 x 6.5". *Courtesy of P.H.P. Hall Of Frames*, Value $275-$325.

ART NOUVEAU, ca. 1905. A European hand carved wooden frame showing the soft lines of the Art Nouveau style. The carving was called "chip carving." This was designed for a cabinet card. 7.25 x 10.5" with a picture size of 4.25 x 6.5". *Courtesy of P.H.P. Hall Of Frames*, Value $300-$325.

ART NOUVEAU, The style is ca. 1905. The Art Nouveau frame is an English reproduction, made well after 1905. It is marked "Bristol" and is a very nice reproduction. It can sell for about $175. 6 x 11". *Courtesy of P.H.P. Hall Of Frames.*

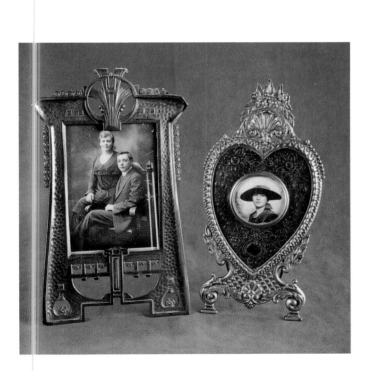

ART NOUVEAU AND VICTORIAN, ca. 1905. The brass frame on the left has the soft Art Nouveau lines. This was made to hold a cabinet card. 6.5 x 11" with a picture size of 4.25 x 6.5". The right one is a slightly later, probably English, Victorian frame made of brass with a copper center moulding. 6 x 10". *Courtesy of P.H.P. Hall Of Frames*, Value (L-R) $200-$250, $275-$325.

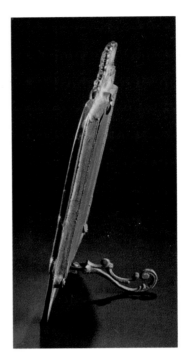

ART NOUVEAU, ca. 1905. A brass or bronze Art Nouveau frame with a woman's head design in the center top. The back of the frame has a pivot stand which was used from the 1890s to the 1920s. 6.5 x 10" with a picture size of 4.25 x 6.5", a cabinet card size. *Courtesy of P.H.P. Hall Of Frames*, Value $250-300.

ART NOUVEAU, ca. 1905. A brass Art Nouveau frame with a pivot stand. 5.5 x 9.25" with a picture size of 4.25 x 6.5", a cabinet card size. *Courtesy of P.H.P. Hall Of Frames*, Value $250-300.

ART NOUVEAU, ca. 1905. A brass Art Nouveau frame with an African woman's head design in the center top. The back of the frame has a pivot stand. 3.75 x 5" with a picture size of 2.75 x 2.5". Most table top frames allow room for a picture that is taller than it is wide. This frame is unusual in that it does not follow that practice. *Courtesy of P.H.P. Hall Of Frames*, Value $250-300.

ART NOUVEAU, ca. 1905. The frame on the left is silver plated metal and the one on the right is brass plated cast iron with a pivoting leg. (L-R) 6 x 8.5" and 6.75 x 10". *Courtesy of P.H.P. Hall Of Frames*, Value (L-R) $225-$275, $325-$375.

ART NOUVEAU, ca. 1905 and 1910. The Art Nouveau frame on the left is a very attractive frame with its soft curves and swirls. Copies are being made today and you must look closely at the finish. The design should be crisp and smooth. Copies may lack the crisp edges and the finish may be coarse. The brass frame on the right is a simple French style. (L-R) 8.25 x 4.5", 2.75 x 4.75". *Courtesy of P.H.P. Hall Of Frames*, Value (L-R) $250-$300, $100-$125.

ART NOUVEAU BRONZE, ca. 1905. This handsome tapered bronze frame has distinct Art Nouveau styling, such as the gentle taper of the frame and the embellishment at the bottom center of the frame. It was probably made in France or England. 5.5 x 9". Value $250-$300.

BRASS, ca. 1905. An English brass frame with a stylized wall frame effect. 5.25 x 7.25". *Courtesy of P.H.P. Hall Of Frames*, Value $150-$200.

NOUVEAU, ca. 1905. A brass plated cast iron frame with sunflowers. A pivoting leg swings out from the rear. 8 x 13.5". *Courtesy of P.H.P. Hall Of Frames*, Value $275-$325.

LIBERTY, ca. 1905. A hand hammered copper on wood "Tulip" framed mirror sold by Liberty & Co. of London. 25" tall x 14" at the top and 15.5" at the bottom. Value $1,200-$1,350. *Courtesy of Zeigeist Antiques.*

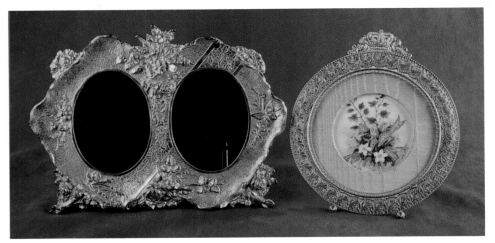

IRON AND BRASS, ca. 1905 and 1915. The double frame on the left is made of brass plated cast iron. The other is a French style brass circular frame. (L-R) 10 x 12" and 8 x 9.25". *Courtesy of P.H.P. Hall Of Frames*, Value (L-R) $275-$325, $125-$175.

POSTCARD, ca. 1905. A wonderful small paperboard "gate style" frame marked "copyright 1905 W.S. Heal." This style of frame could be found at seaside resorts as souvenirs of your stay at the resort. It has an easel back and a hook for hanging on the wall. 7 x 9" with a picture size of 3.5 x 5.25". Value $50-$70.

ART NOUVEAU INFLUENCE, 1908. An English (Birmingham) sterling silver frame with Art Nouveau soft lines, curved glass, and engraving. The hallmark dates it to 1908. The silver is mounted on an oak back. This style of frame is being copied in England with the copies having an almost mylar looking plain silver plated face and a simple wooden back. 5.25 x 7.75" with a picture size of 4 x 5.75". Value $300-$350.

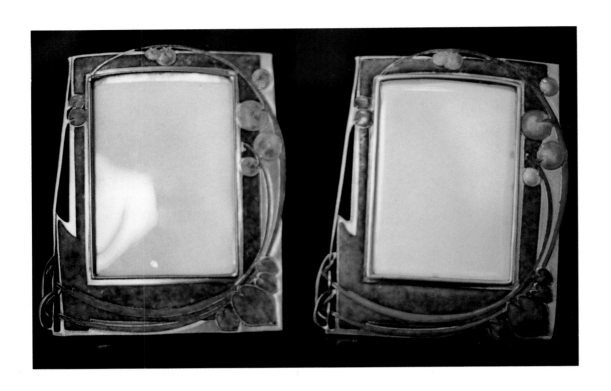

LIBERTY, ca. 1906. Two incredible silver gilt and hand enameled frames sold by Liberty & Co. of London. The design was by Archibald Knox, Liberty's finest designer, and the enamel work is slightly different on each. 5.5 x 9". Value $40,000-$55,000 for the pair. *Courtesy of John Jesse Antiques.*

ENGLISH, ca. 1910. Heavy bronze ornate frame made in England. On the back side, the pivoting clips used to put in or remove the photo were not made after 1925. 7.75 x 12.5" with a picture size of 4.25 x 6". This frame has been recently reproduced with the reproduction having a silver plated finish. *Courtesy of P.H.P. Hall Of Frames*, Value $500-$600 (original).

ORNATE BRASS, ca. 1910. Heavy brass ornate frame made in England. 6.5 x 9.75" with a picture size of 4.5 x 6". *Courtesy of P.H.P. Hall Of Frames*, Value $250-$300.

CAST IRON, ca. 1910. A heavy gold painted cast iron cherub and flowers design frame with a swinging leg stand. 4.75 x 7.5". This may be a current reproduction of an earlier frame or a recent discovery of old unsold stock. Everything looks right, but the seller of this and other similar frames had loads of them and was selling them for about $20 each. Either the buyers were getting great bargains or these are exceptionally good reproductions. Value $85-$115, if old.

ORNATE BRONZE, ca. 1910. Heavy bronze ornate frame made in England. 4.5 x 7.5" with a picture size of 2.5 x 3.75". *Courtesy of P.H.P. Hall Of Frames*, Value $350-$400.

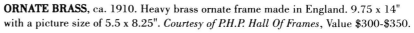

ORNATE BRASS, ca. 1910. Heavy brass ornate frame made in England. 9.75 x 14" with a picture size of 5.5 x 8.25". *Courtesy of P.H.P. Hall Of Frames*, Value $300-$350.

ORNATE BRASS, ca. 1910. Silver plated brass frame with applied metal flowers made in England. 6.75 x 11.5" with a picture size of 5.25 x 7.5". *Courtesy of P.H.P. Hall Of Frames*, Value $200-$300.

MOSAIC, ca. 1910. A mosaic design created with a flat glass cane laid into a wooden frame made in Murano, Italy. 8 x 11.5" with a picture size of 4.5 x 5.5". *Courtesy of P.H.P. Hall Of Frames*, Value $500-$600.

MOSAIC, ca. 1910. A mosaic design created with a flat and raised glass cane laid surrounded by a twisted brass ribbon made in Murano, Italy. 4 x 5" with a picture size of 3.25 x 2.25". *Courtesy of P.H.P. Hall Of Frames*, Value $450-$500.

CAST IRON, ca. 1910. A heavy cast iron leaf design frame with a swinging leg stand. 9 x 12" with a picture size of 4.25 x 6". Value $75-$110.

MOSAIC, ca. 1910. A mosaic design created with a flat and raised glass cane laid into a wooden frame surrounded by a flat brass ribbon made in Murano, Italy. The side view shows where the easel back is attached. 3.75 x 4.5" with a picture size of 2 x 3". *Courtesy of P.H.P. Hall Of Frames*, Value $450-$500.

MOSAIC, ca. 1910. Three tiny table top frames with a mosaic design created with a flat and raised glass cane laid into a wooden frame made in Murano, Italy. Each frame is only 2" tall and the widths vary from 1.5 to 2.25". *Courtesy of P.H.P. Hall Of Frames*, Value $150-$225.

MOSAIC, ca. 1910. A tiny table top frame with a mosaic design created with a flat and raised glass cane made in Murano, Italy. 2.5 x 3.25". *Courtesy of P.H.P. Hall Of Frames*, Value $200-$225.

BRASS, ca. 1910. A French style brass frame with crossed swords. 5 x 9". *Courtesy of P.H.P. Hall Of Frames*, Value $150-$200.

BRASS, ca. 1910. Three French, well made small frames. The left and center are brass while the right one is of bronze. (L-R) 2 x 4.25", 2.25 x 4.75" and 2.5 x 4.25". *Courtesy of P.H.P. Hall Of Frames*, Value $150-$175 each.

BRASS, ca. 1910. Two brass frames with swirling floral boarders. The one on the right has beveled glass. (L-R) 6.5 x 12" and 5 x 8.5". *Courtesy of P.H.P. Hall Of Frames*, Value (L-R) $275-$325, $225-$275.

CAST IRON, ca. 1910. A heavy cast iron Palmer Cox Brownie design frame with a hair pin tray. 4.5 x 6". This may be a current reproduction of an earlier frame or a recent discovery of old unsold stock. Everything looks right, but the seller of this and other similar frames had loads of them and was selling them very reasonably. Either the buyers were getting great bargains or these are exceptionally good reproductions. Value $300-$350, if old.

BRASS WIRE, ca. 1910. A French brass wire frame with a small enamel portrait button and two stones at the bottom. 5.75 x 9.25". *Courtesy of P.H.P. Hall Of Frames*, Value $285-$335.

ENGLISH BRASS, ca. 1910. A small photo in an extended frame. 6 x 8".
Courtesy of P.H.P. Hall Of Frames, Value $225-$275.

THREE SECTION, ca. 1910. A triple brass frame edged in a swirling floral pattern. 7.5 x 10.5". *Courtesy of P.H.P. Hall Of Frames*, Value $375-$425.

BRASS WIRE, ca. 1910. A French brass wire frame with flower accents. 8 x 12". *Courtesy of P.H.P. Hall Of Frames*, Value $275-$325.

BRASS, ca. 1910. The frame on the left has elements of the Art Nouveau period with its soft curves and turned over edges, while the frame on the right is more traditional. 3.75 x 4.25" and 3.75 x 6.75. *Courtesy of P.H.P. Hall Of Frames*, Value (L-R) $225-$275, $95-$125.

BRASS AND ENAMEL, ca. 1910. An Indian cast brass frame. 6 x 7.5". Value $150-$175.

BRONZE, ca. 1910. This frame is unusual with its landscape (horizontal) orientation. 4.5 x 6.5". *Courtesy of P.H.P. Hall Of Frames*, Value $225-$275.

BIRCH WOOD, ca. 1910. A birch wood frame from Sweden. 4.25 x 7.5". Value $75-$95.

BIRCH WOOD, ca. 1910. A birch wood frame from Sweden in a harder to find horizontal format. 6 x 7". Value $85-$110.

BRASS, ca. 1910, 1918, 1896. Three small frames. The left and center are brass while the right one is of copper. (L-R) 2.75 x 2.75", 4.75 x 6", and 2 x 3.5". *Courtesy of P.H.P. Hall Of Frames*, Value (L-R) $50-$75, $175-$225, $150-$175.

THREE FRAMES, ca. 1910, 1900, and 1930. The frame on the left is cast iron with hand painted blue highlights. It is 6.25 x 10.5". The center frame is silver coated metal with an ivy design. The right frame is a white metal with a leaf and vine design. *Courtesy of P.H.P. Hall Of Frames*, Value (L-R) $200-$250, $175-$225, $125-$175.

BRASS CIRCLE, ca. 1915. Almost a patriotic nude stands beside the opening for the photograph of a loved one. Probably made in France. 5.5" in diameter. Value $200-$250.

RIBBONS, CHERUBS, AND ANGELS, ca. 1915. A superbly executed small French frame with a ribbon top and distinguished cherubs and angels at the sides and bottom. 5.5 x 4". Value $300-$350.

INLAID, ca. 1915. A floral pattern inlaid into wood. The inlays can be bone, ivory, or mother-of-pearl. 8.5 x 12" with a picture size of 6.75 x 8.5". *Courtesy of P.H.P. Hall Of Frames*, Value $250-$300.

ENAMEL AND MOSAIC, ca. 1915. A micro mosaic design surrounded by enamel. 3.25 x 4.5" with a picture size of 2.5 x 3.75". *Courtesy of P.H.P. Hall Of Frames*, Value $300-$400.

BRASS, ca. 1915. Two simple, small brass frames. These simple frames are common. (L-R) 2.5 x 3.5" and 2.5 x 3.75". *Courtesy of P.H.P. Hall Of Frames*, Value $50-$75 each.

GROUP OF FOUR, ca. 1915. A French style brass, hinged set of four frames. Each frame is 1.75 x 2.75". *Courtesy of P.H.P. Hall Of Frames*, Value $175-$225.

ARTS AND CRAFTS, ca. 1915. A simple Arts and Crafts style frame, hand-made and set with stones. 3.75 x 4". *Courtesy of P.H.P. Hall Of Frames*, Value $275-$325.

BRASS OVAL, ca. 1915. Two brass frames. (L-R) 4.75 x 8" and 5.5 x 7". *Courtesy of P.H.P. Hall Of Frames*, Value $100-$150.

BRASS WALL FRAME STYLE, ca. 1915. A baroque style frame that looks better from the front than the back. The back shows that the stamped out frame is less than high quality. 5 x 5.75". *Courtesy of P.H.P. Hall Of Frames*, Value $80-$100.

BRASS WALL FRAME STYLE, ca. 1915. A picture frame style with nice high detail. 5.75 x 7.5". *Courtesy of P.H.P. Hall Of Frames*, Value $250-$300.

BRASS, ca. 1915. The frame on the left is English and the top decoration is a later added piece. The frame on the right has cherubs and French fleur de lis designs. (L-R) 7.25 x 10.5" and 6.5 x 10". *Courtesy of P.H.P. Hall Of Frames*, Value $275-$325 each.

GOLD PLATED WITH ENAMEL HIGHLIGHTS, ca. 1915. A gold plated brass frame with enamel detail. 4.25 x 6.5". *Courtesy of P.H.P. Hall Of Frames*, Value $275-$325.

BRASS WALL FRAME STYLE, ca. 1915. A picture frame style showing nice detail. 7.5 x 9.5". *Courtesy of P.H.P. Hall Of Frames*, Value $225-$275.

ARTS AND CRAFTS, ca. 1915. This brass frame has elements of the Art Nouveau period with its soft curves but has the traditional simplicity of the handmade Arts and Crafts object. 3.75 x 3.75". *Courtesy of P.H.P. Hall Of Frames*, Value $175-$225.

MORROCAN WOOD, ca. 1920. A tremendous amount of hand work has gone into this frame. Each star is made up of tiny chips of ivory with mother-of-pearl. Between the inlays, the maker has incised a repeating floral design. 8 x 10.25" with a picture size of 4.25 x 6.5", a cabinet card size. *Courtesy of P.H.P. Hall Of Frames*, Value $200-$250.

BRASS, ca. 1920. An English table top frame with a traditional design. 7.5 x 9.75" with a picture size of 5.75 x 8". *Courtesy of P.H.P. Hall Of Frames*, Value $150-$225.

SILVER, ca. 1920. Two English compact style table top frames. (L) 2.125 x 2.5" and (R) 1.875 x 2.5". *Courtesy of P.H.P. Hall Of Frames*, Value $175-$225 each.

MINIATURE, ca. 1920. Two small French frames. Both are made of brass. The one on the right is set with rhinestones. 1.5 x 2". *Courtesy of P.H.P. Hall Of Frames*, Value $60-$100 each.

MINIATURE, ca. 1920. Two small frames, one of wood and the other made of brass. The one on the left is a miniature version of the typical walnut oval so popular after the Civil War. The one on the right is a traditional French style frame. 2 x 2.75". *Courtesy of P.H.P. Hall Of Frames*, Value (L) $60-$100, (R) $150-$175.

BALL FOOT, ca. 1920. A delicate French frame made of brass. 2 x 4.125". *Courtesy of P.H.P. Hall Of Frames*, Value $150-$200.

LINKING RING, ca. 1920. This English frame is made of brass. The use of linking rings was a popular style for Victorian frames and this refined version shows how rings were used after the turn of the century. 3.5 x 4.75". *Courtesy of P.H.P. Hall Of Frames*, Value $130-$200.

GRAPE MOTIF, ca. 1920. This French silver plated frame has bunches of grapes surrounding a fabric interior. The cover glass in domed. This is a very attractive frame. 5.125 x 6.125". *Courtesy of P.H.P. Hall Of Frames*, Value $300-$400.

BRASS, ca. 1920. Two small frames, both probably made in England. Dating can be difficult with these frames as the style was popular from about 1910 to 1930. (L-R) 2.375 x 3.5" and 1.25 x 2.625". *Courtesy of P.H.P. Hall Of Frames*, Value $60-$100 each.

ENAMEL, ca. 1920. Three small frames with applied enamel work. (L-R) 2 x 2.25", 1.75 x 2.25", and 1.375 x 2". *Courtesy of P.H.P. Hall Of Frames*, Value $100-$170 each.

TWISTED WIRE, ca. 1920. A simple round frame using a double twisted wire as the outer moulding. These are not difficult to find. 4.5 x 4.5". *Courtesy of P.H.P. Hall Of Frames*, Value $100-$150.

BRASS, ca. 1920. Two brass frames. 3.5 x 4.75" and 3.5 x 5". *Courtesy of P.H.P. Hall Of Frames*, Value $150-$200.

BRASS WITH STONES, ca. 1920. This simple easel back brass frame is enhanced by the placing of blue faceted rhinestones at the corners. The size is 4 x 6". Value $85-$95.

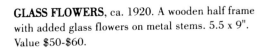

GLASS FLOWERS, ca. 1920. A wooden half frame with added glass flowers on metal stems. 5.5 x 9". Value $50-$60.

THREE LEGGED TABLE, ca. 1920. A very unusual frame of a silver metal in the shape of a small three legged table with a tilting top. 4" tall. Value $250-$300. *Courtesy of John Jesse Antiques.*

BAMBOO AND WOOD, ca. 1920. An interesting frame composed of several woods with a bamboo outer rim. 5 x 7". Value $100-$125.

WOOD AND WIRE ORIENTAL, ca. 1920. The Indian image on the frame is inlaid silver wire. 5 x 7". Value $110-$125.

AUSTRIAN, ca. 1920. A silver plated frame with hand set Austrian stones. 4 x 5.25". *Courtesy of P.H.P. Hall Of Frames*, Value $250-$300.

WOOD, ca. 1920. A wooden frame with incised exotic woods, mother-of-pearl, and ivory. 4.25 x 5.25". *Courtesy of P.H.P. Hall Of Frames*, Value $225-$275.

AUSTRIAN, ca. 1920. Silver plated frames, hand set Austrian stones. The frame on the left has a Victorian style palette on an easel. (L-R) 4 x 6", 3 x 3.25". *Courtesy of P.H.P. Hall Of Frames*, Value (L-R) $250-$300, $225-$275.

CHERUBS, ca. 1920. Two brass frames. The frame on the left is either English or French. It has an outer edge of flying cherubs and an inner edge of roses. The frame on the right is French and has cherubs, forget-me-nots, and roses in the moulding with a "French ribbon" at the top. (L-R) 2 x 3.75", 3 x 4.5". *Courtesy of P.H.P. Hall Of Frames*, Value (L-R) $225-$275, $225-$275.

AUSTRIAN, ca. 1920. A brass frame in an Irish harp pattern with hand set Austrian stones. 8.5 x 11". *Courtesy of P.H.P. Hall Of Frames*, Value $375-$425.

AUSTRIAN, ca. 1920. A brass frame with hand set Austrian stones. 7.5 x 9.5". *Courtesy of P.H.P. Hall Of Frames*, Value $350-$400.

BRASS, ca. 1920. Three relatively simple, well made brass frames. The left frame uses the wall frame design while the other two have an interlocking swirled leaf design. (L-R) 5.25 x 7", 5.25 x 7.25", and 4.75 x 6.5". *Courtesy of P.H.P. Hall Of Frames*, Value $150-$175 each.

MEXICAN SILVER PLATE, ca. 1920. A silver plated frame marked "Manufactured and plated by Simpson A. Mexico-USA 638". 8.5 x 11". *Courtesy of P.H.P. Hall Of Frames*, Value $225-$275.

CHINESE WOOD, ca. 1920. A great intricate wooden hand carved frame. The quality of the carving is very good. 10 x 15". *Courtesy of P.H.P. Hall Of Frames*, Value $225-$275.

BRASS, ca. 1920. A simple brass frame with detailed edge and beveled glass. 10 x 12". *Courtesy of P.H.P. Hall Of Frames*, Value $135-$175.

BRASS, ca. 1920. An brass frame with an Egyptian motif. The discovery of King Tut's tomb inspired the adoption of all things Egyptian. 3.5 x 6". Value $100-$135.

TINY, ca. 1925. A small brass frame. 2 x 2.25". *Courtesy of P.H.P. Hall Of Frames,* Value $90-$125.

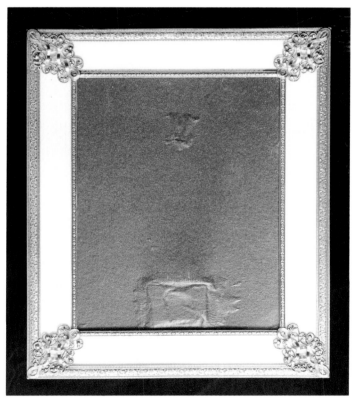

WEDDING FRAME, ca. 1925. An elegant American brass wedding picture frame with love knot designs at the corners. It has a machine engraved edge pattern that also appears on the outer sides of the frame and a velveteen covered board back and easel with hooks for hanging on the wall. 10 x 12" with a picture size of 7 x 9". Value $175-$200.

HANGING OR TABLE TOP FRAME, ca. 1925. An American brass frame with double corners. It has a machine engraved edge and a velveteen covered board back and easel with a hook for hanging on the wall. 4.25 x 5.25" with a picture size of 2.25 x 3.5". Value $95-$125.

LEATHER, ca. 1920 and 1930. Two leather frames, tooled and hand painted. The frame on the left is earlier. (L-R) 9 x 12", Value $175-$225; and 8.5 x 10.5", made in Italy, *Courtesy of P.H.P. Hall Of Frames*, Value $100-$150.

SWIVEL, ca. 1925. A simple, two sided small brass frame. 2.75 x 3.5". *Courtesy of P.H.P. Hall Of Frames*, Value $225-$250 each.

ENGLISH BRASS, ca. 1930 and 1910. The frame on the left is a heavy cast brass in an ivy vine pattern and the right frame was made by "Simpson" in a different leaf pattern. 4.5 x 5.5" and 4 x 5". *Courtesy of P.H.P. Hall Of Frames*, Value (L-R) $100-$125 and $150-$175.

SWING, ca. 1928. An Art Deco flavored frame that swings on the two outer pillars. There are hundreds of these painted or decorated wood swing frames available to the collector. The prices are very reasonable. 8.25 x 8.5" with a picture size of 5 x 7". Value $20-$40.

SCANDINAVIAN, ca. 1930 and 1910. Two beautiful frames in wood, made in Scandinavia. The frame on the left has an Art Deco flavor and the frame at right is more traditional. 7.75 x 5.25" and 5.25 x 7.5". *Courtesy of P.H.P. Hall Of Frames*, Value (L-R) $175-$225, $145-$175.

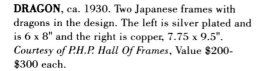

MOSAIC, ca. 1930. A micro mosaic design created with a tiny pieces of flat glass cane made in Murano, Italy. (L-R) 2.5 x 4.25" and 5 x 7". *Courtesy of P.H.P. Hall Of Frames*, Value $200-$250 each.

DRAGON, ca. 1930. Two Japanese frames with dragons in the design. The left is silver plated and is 6 x 8" and the right is copper, 7.75 x 9.5". *Courtesy of P.H.P. Hall Of Frames*, Value $200-$300 each.

IVORY, ca. 1930. A small carved ivory frame with pierced and carved floral design. The quality of the carving is not very good. 1.25 x 2.25". *Courtesy of P.H.P. Hall Of Frames*, Value $70-$90.

BROACH, ca. 1930. A sterling silver frame that can be worn as a broach. 1.25 x 1.75". *Courtesy of P.H.P. Hall Of Frames*, Value $60-$100.

BRASS, ca. 1930. The frame on the left is European in silver plated brass and has a simple beaded edge with applied corners. The frame on the right is unusual as it is pewter and has a sea barnacle raised design. It is marked "Metzke" as the maker. (L-R) 3.75 x 6", 4 x 5". *Courtesy of P.H.P. Hall Of Frames*, Value (L-R) $60-$90, $150-$200.

BLACK GLASS, ca. 1930. Brass filigree work on a background of black glass gives this frame an 1860s look. 3.5 x 4.75".
Courtesy of P.H.P. Hall Of Frames, Value $275-$325.

ART DECO, ca. 1936. Heavy aircraft or zeppelin aluminum with a hand wrought back and stand. The back is marked "Palmer Smith" makers. Actively sought by Art Deco collectors. 8.5 x 10.5" with a picture size of 8 x 10". Value $150-$200.

BRONZE, ca. 1935. Two table top frames in bronze metal. 7.5 x 9.5" and 8.25 x 10.5". *Courtesy of P.H.P. Hall Of Frames*, Value $100-$150.

PLASTIC, ca. 1937. An early thermoplastic frame. The overall effect is that of abalone or mother-of-pearl. 5 x 5". *Courtesy of P.H.P. Hall Of Frames*, Value $120-$145.

BRASS STEPS TO THE CATHEDRAL, ca. 1938. An unusual frame of stamped brass, ideally designed for a wedding photo of the couple leaving the church. Approximately 7 x 8" with a picture size of approximately 4 x 5". Value $45-$55.

STAMPED BRASS, ca. 1940. A table top frame with flowers in the design. The reverse side shows nice finishing touches not usually found on stamped pieces. 10.5 x 13" with a picture size of 6 x 9". *Courtesy of P.H.P. Hall Of Frames*, Value $75-$100.

PLASTIC, ca. 1940. An early plastic frame with decorated and pierced corners. The overall effect is that of a small ivory frame. 3 x 4". *Courtesy of P.H.P. Hall Of Frames*, Value $45-$75.

BRASS OVAL, ca. 1940. This style of case has been used since the beginning of the 19th century—a brass oval with a hanging hook in a leather covered, velvet, or satin lined case. In this case, dating was achieved by the Bachrach photo contained in the case. 4.5 x 5.5". *Courtesy of P.H.P. Hall Of Frames*, Value $60-80.

WORLD WAR II, ca. 1944. During the Second World War, a "Home Front" movement leant support to our men in arms. This patriotic outpouring shows up in many home goods that come close to being called kitsch. Here is a plaster frame that shows our fighting men. The photo that originally came with the frame (and helped sell the frame) was of Clark Gable in uniform. 7 x 9". Value $75-$100.

WORLD WAR II, ca. 1944. A plaster frame with a soldier. The photo that originally came with the frame (and helped sell the frame) was of Gary Cooper in uniform. 8 x 8". Value $75-$100.

WORLD WAR II, ca. 1944. Reverse painting on glass, this group of three frames shows some of the patriotic designs available during the war years. Each has a an easel back and a hook for hanging. (Two flags) 7 x 9", (two flags and a V) 4.5 x 6.5", and (V with eagle) 8 x 10". Value $35-$65.

TRENCH ART, ca. 1944. During the First World War, soldiers would often be holed up in a trench for months at a time. Some would scavenge for brass shells, and using common tools, would make souvenirs of their time in the trenches. There are many forms of trench art such as cigarette lighters, letter openers, lamps, tables, and picture frames. Local craftsmen got in on the production and sold the art to soldiers leaving for home. This art form was carried on to the Second World War. Local craftsmen would salvage shells and make useful items. This is a picture frame made from large caliber machine gun shells and wood. 10.5 x 14.25". Value $150-$175.

SILK SCREEN PAINTED GLASS, ca. 1944. A glass frame with cardboard back and metal corners. 10 x 12" with a picture size of 7 x 9". Value $25-$40.

WORLD WAR II, ca. 1944. Two patriotic glass frames with cardboard backs and metal clips. 6 x 4.5" and 3 x 3.5". These were popular inexpensive frames sold in the mid-1940s. Value $25-$40.

SILK SCREEN PAINTED GLASS, ca. 1944. Glass frames with cardboard backs and metal corners or clips. Approximately 4 x 5" with a picture size of approximately 2.5 x 3.25". Value $25-$35.

BLUE GLASS, ca. 1948. Two blue glass frames with cardboard backs and metal corners. 4 x 5" with a picture size of 2.5 x 3.5". The blue glass items were popular from about 1948 to 1953. Value $25-$40.

ENAMEL, ca. 1948. The piece on the left is sterling silver with enamel work. The piece on the right is a wire and enamel work called "champleve." Both pieces were made in France. 2.75 x 3.75" and 4.125 x 6.25. *Courtesy of P.H.P. Hall Of Frames*, Value (L-R) $275-$325, 375-$425.

Bibliography

The Frame in America 1860-1960. Catalog of the exhibit of the Federal Reserve Board in Washington, D.C., 1995.

Grimm, Claus. *The Book Of Picture Frames.* Norwalk, Connecticut: Abaris Books, 1992.

Heydenryk, H. *The Art And History Of Frames.* New York: Lyons & Burford, 1993.

Maryanski, Richard. *Antique Picture Frame Guide.* Niles, Illinois: Cedar Forest Co., 1973.

Stephenson, Sue Honaker. *Rustic Furniture.* New York: Van Nostrand Rheinhold Co., 1979.

Wilner, Eli. *Antique American Frames.* New York: Avon Books, 1995.

Resources

P.H.P. Hall of Frames. Helpful and knowledgeable dealers in fine table top frames. No shop, but you can find them at major New York shows or call to tell them your wants. Tel. 212-928-6805.

Zeitgeist Antiques. Arts and Crafts and Art Nouveau items. 58 Kensington Church St., London W8 4DB, England. Tel./fax 0171 938-4817.

John Jesse Antiques. 20th Century Decorative Arts, super high quality. 160 Kensington Church St., London, W8 4BN. Tel. 0171 229-0312, fax 0171 229-4732.

Hayman & Hayman. Antique Photograph Frames, probably the best source of early table top frames in London. You can find them at Antiquarius, booth K3, 135 King's Rd., London, SW3 4PW. Tel. 0171 351-6568, fax 0181 563 0582.

Portobello Road Antiques. Nice selection of unusual items and frames, 491 Grand Ave., Englewood, NJ 07631. Tel. 201-568-5559, fax 201-568-1568.

Index

V

velvet, 10, 17, 49, 70, 78
veneer, 9, 13, 14, 17, 19, 23, 24,
    26, 27, 36-40, 44
Victorian, 10-12, 19, 70, 74, 78,
    104, 116, 128, 147, 152
vulcanized, 41

W

Walnut, 9, 14, 17, 24, 25, 37, 43,
    45, 48, 51, 52, 56-58, 65, 88
water gilding   , 14, 25, 50
wedding, 19, 155, 164
White, Stanford, 10, 11
windows, 11
wire, 12, 17, 19, 103, 104, 121,
    136, 137, 149, 150
World War, 11, 89, 167-169, 171

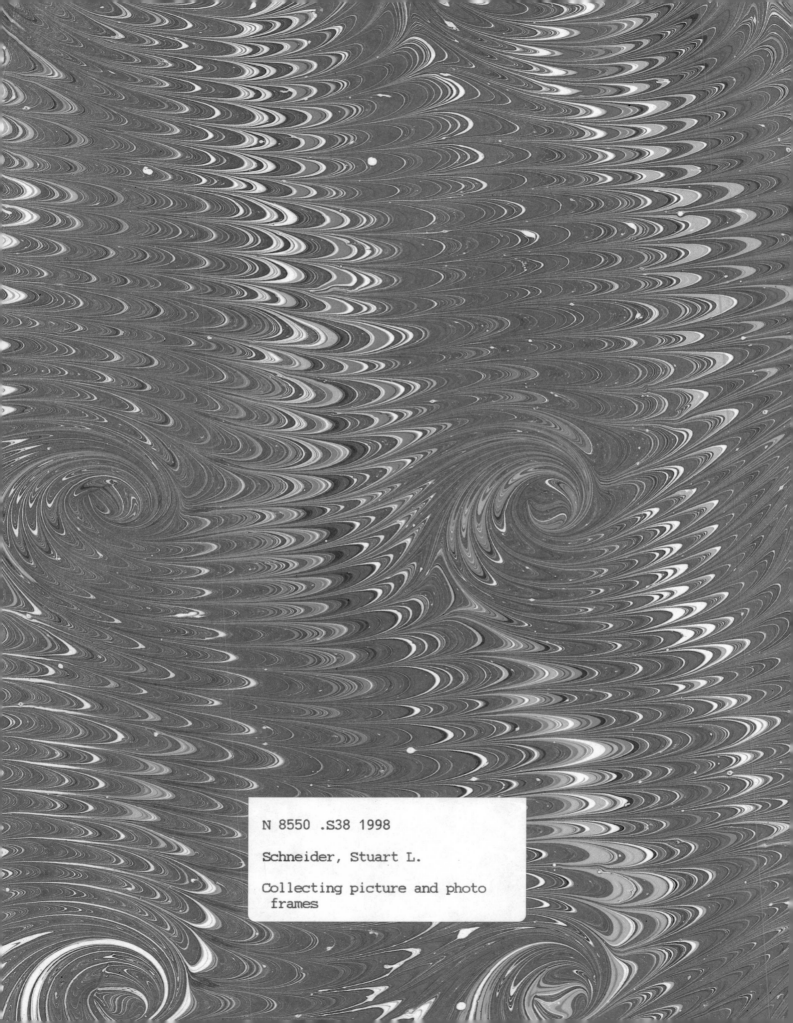